AA/Baedeker
New York

Baedeker's

AA

New York

THE AUTOMOBILE ASSOCIATION

Imprint

Cover picture: World Trade Center

78 colour photographs
23 plans, 3 plans of bus routes, 1 large city map

Text and selection of illustrations:
Carin Drechsler-Marx

Conception and editorial work:
Redaktionsbüro Harenberg, Schwerte
English language: Alec Court

Cartography:
Georg Schiffner, Lahr

General direction:
Dr Peter Baumgarten, Baedeker Stuttgart

English translation: James Hogarth

Source of illustrations:
Drechsler-Marx (66), United States Travel Service (3), Historia-Photo (5), Mauritius (1), Uthoff (3)

Following the tradition established by Karl Baedeker in 1844, sights of particular interest and hotels of particular quality are distinguished by either one or two asterisks.

To make it easier to locate the various sights listed in the "A to Z" section of the Guide, their coordinates on the large city map of New York are shown in red at the head of each entry.

Only a selection of hotels and restaurants can be given: no reflection is implied, therefore, on establishments not included.

In a time of rapid change it is difficult to ensure that all the information given is entirely accurate and up to date, and the possibility of error can never be entirely eliminated. Although the publishers can accept no responsibility for inaccuracies and omissions they are always grateful for corrections and suggestions for improvement.

2nd Edition 1984

© Baedeker Stuttgart
Original German edition

© Jarrold and Sons Ltd
English language edition worldwide

© The Automobile Association 1982 57134
United Kingdom and Ireland

Licensed user:
Mairs Geographischer Verlag GmbH & Co., Ostfildern-Kemnat bei Stuttgart

Reproductions:
Gölz Repro-Service GmbH, Ludwigsburg

The name *Baedeker* is a registered trademark

Printed in Great Britain by Jarrold and Sons Ltd
Norwich

ISBN 0 86145 118 x

Contents

	Page
The Principal Sights at a Glance . . . . inside front cover	
Preface	7
Facts and Figures	9
General	9
Population and Religion	9
Transport	12
Culture	14
Commerce and Industry	15
Notable New Yorkers	17
History of New York	22
Quotations	27
New York from A to Z	30
Practical Information	112
Useful Telephone Numbers at a Glance	167
City Map . . . . at end of book	

Preface

This Pocket Guide to New York is one of the new generation of Baedeker guides.

These pocket-sized city guides, illustrated throughout in colour, are designed to meet the needs of the modern traveller. They are quick and easy to consult, with the principal sights described in alphabetical order and practical details about opening times, how to get there, etc., shown in the margin.

Each guide is divided into three parts. The first part gives a general account of the city, its history, population, culture and so on; in the second part its principal sights are described; and the third part contains a variety of practical information designed to help visitors to find their way about and make the most of their stay. For the reader's convenience this practical information, like the main part of the guide, is arranged in alphabetical order.

The new guides are abundantly illustrated and contain numbers of newly drawn plans. In a pocket at the back of the book is a large city map, and each entry in the main part of the guide gives the coordinates of the square on the map in which the particular building or feature is situated. Users of this guide, therefore, will have no difficulty in finding what they want to see.

Facts and Figures

Arms of the City
of New York

General

Although New York is the largest city in the United States and one of the largest cities in the world it is not the national capital, nor even the capital of New York State, more than two-fifths of whose inhabitants live in the city. It lies in the NE of the country – the oldest part of the United States – around the mouth of the Hudson River, which here flows into the Atlantic Ocean. More precisely, it lies in latitude 40°42′26″ N and longitude 74°0′23″ W.

New York City reached its present extent in 1898 with the formation of Greater New York, which has an area of 829 sq. km (320 sq. miles). Its present population is over 7 million. A further 8 million live in the economic region around the city, the New York Metropolitan Area, which takes in Westchester, Rockland and Nassau counties in New York State, the southern tip of Connecticut and the northern part of New Jersey.

Area and population

The city is made up of five boroughs, of which Manhattan is the smallest in area (57 sq. km – 22 sq. miles) and the third largest in population. The other boroughs are Brooklyn (210 sq. km – 81 sq. miles), Bronx (107 sq. km – 41 sq. miles), Queens (308 sq. km – 119 sq. miles) and Staten Island (150 sq. km – 58 sq. miles). Only Bronx is on the mainland: the other four boroughs are on islands, with Brooklyn and Queens occupying the south-western end of Long Island, which extends NE for some 200 km (125 miles).

The boroughs

The city's administration is run by the Mayor, who is elected for a four-year term, the 39-member City Council, also elected every four years, and the Board of Estimate, a kind of second chamber in which the Mayor, the president of the City Council and the comptroller (city treasurer) each have three votes and the presidents of the five boroughs each have two votes.

Administration

The levying of new taxes and the passing of new laws in certain fields require the authorisation of the New York State legislature, which meets in the state capital of Albany, some 200 km (125 miles) up the Hudson.

Population and Religion

During the 200 years after the first settlement of Manhattan the town developed very slowly, and by the beginning of the 18th c. it had no more than 5000 inhabitants. By 1790 this had risen to 33,000, and in the following ten years this figure almost doubled. Soon New York displaced Philadelphia as the largest town in America, but it was not until the period of mass

Population

◀ *Statue of Liberty*

immigration in the second half of the 19th c. that the population passed the million mark. In the years up to the First World War the immigrants consisted mainly of Irish, Germans (a quarter of a million in the record year of 1882), Italians and Jews from Eastern Europe, with smaller numbers of English and Scottish, Polish and Ukrainian, Czech and Hungarian immigrants. The numbers were much reduced after 1924 when immigration quotas were introduced.

Between 1933 and 1942, and again after the end of the Second World War, New York became a place of refuge for people seeking safety from Nazi persecution or escape from the hardships of the post-war years. During the war there was also a considerable influx of negroes from the southern states, seeking employment and better pay in New York and other north-eastern cities; and this movement continued after the end of the war, when the increasing mechanisation of agriculture in the southern states led to the loss of many jobs. There was also an increasing inflow of Spanish-speaking immigrants, particularly from the American territory of Puerto Rico but also from the Caribbean and Central and South America. There are now more than a million Puerto Ricans in New York – more than in their own capital of San Juan – and Spanish has become the city's second language. The proportion of negroes in the population of New York has risen to 22%; in Manhattan it is exactly a quarter.

Ethnic variety

This immigration has produced an extraordinary variety of ethnic groups in New York, many of them living in their own quarter of the city – Chinese in Chinatown, Italians in Little Italy, Poles and Ukrainians in East Village, Hungarians, Czechs

Manhattan – a bird's-eye view

People of New York

and Germans in East Side, Latin Americans in the Barrio, negroes in Harlem, Dominicans and Cubans on Washington Heights. In addition to these foreign colonies in Manhattan there are others in Brooklyn – Arabs (mainly Syrians and Lebanese) around Atlantic Avenue, Hassidic Jews in Williamsburg, Norwegians in Bay Ridge. In Queens there is a large Greek colony in the district of Astoria, and many Colombians have settled on Jackson Heights. All these various groups have their own shops and restaurants, and frequently also churches in which services are held in their own languages.

New Yorkers of Chinatown

Religion

Well over 100 different religious creeds and denominations are represented in New York, and in Manhattan alone there are something like 650 churches and almost 100 synagogues. Manhattan and Brooklyn are Roman Catholic archiepiscopal dioceses, and Manhattan has a cardinal archbishop. The Episcopalian and the Presbyterian, Methodist and Baptist communities are each of roughly the same size as the Roman Catholics. In addition New York has places of worship belonging to the Quakers, the Mennonites, the Unitarians, the Adventists, the Lutheran and Reformed churches, the Pentecostal movement, the Old Catholics, the Russian and Greek Orthodox churches, the Moravian Brethren, Christian Science and a variety of other sects. There are Buddhist and Hindu temples, mosques and even an (American) Indian church. Some communities, particularly the Roman Catholics and the Jews (orthodox, reform and liberal), run their own schools. Since there is a complete separation of church and state in the USA, all religious communities depend for finance on contributions from their members.

Transport

The port

Although New York possesses a natural harbour in the Hudson River and New York Bay this is no longer of any great importance. Only a few piers in the 50th–60th Street area are still in use for passenger vessels, almost solely engaged in Caribbean cruises; and the amount of freight handled has also fallen, since much of the traffic now passes through the container terminal at Port Elizabeth, across the bay in New Jersey.

New York has three airports – John F. Kennedy (formerly known as Idlewild), which handles international traffic and services to the western states; LaGuardia (named after the popular Mayor of that name), used only by domestic services; and Newark, used by both international and American airlines. The airports are managed by the Port Authority of New York and New Jersey.
The John F. Kennedy International Airport is the largest of the three airports and the farthest from the city centre (26 km – 16 miles). Newark is 25 km (15½ miles) from the city centre, LaGuardia only 13 km (8 miles).

Airports

The long-distance trains running from New York's two main-line stations, Grand Central and Pennsylvania, carry a relatively small proportion of the total traffic, most of which goes by air or bus, but the railways still play an important part in the suburban and commuter traffic to the N and W of the city. Pennsylvania Station is also the terminus of the Long Island Railroad, which carries the heaviest traffic of any suburban line in the United States. There is also the PATH line (the Hudson Tubes), providing connections with New Jersey.
Long-distance and commuter buses leave from the Port Authority Bus Terminal on Eighth Avenue (40th and 41st Streets), where thousands of buses arrive and depart every day.

Rail and bus services

The New York Subway, which serves all the boroughs except Staten Island, has a total track length of some 354 km (220

Subway

TWA terminal for overseas flights, John F. Kennedy Airport

miles), with 23 lines and 462 stations. Running 24 hours a day, it carries a daily total of some 2 million passengers.

Buses and taxis

Much of the city's internal traffic is carried by its network of bus services, with almost 40 routes in Manhattan alone. New York's trams ceased to run in the 1950s.

New York's public transport systems are supplemented by something like 11,000 taxis.

Roads out of New York

The main routes out of New York are:

To New Jersey: Holland Tunnel on Canal Street, Lincoln Tunnel on 34th Street, George Washington Bridge on 181st Street.

To upper New York State and the N: Deegan Expressway through the Bronx, then New York Thruway.

To the New England states: Cross-Bronx Expressway, Bruckner Boulevard, Hutchinson River Parkway.

To Queens and Long Island: Queens-Midtown Tunnel (37th Street), Queensboro Bridge (59th Street), Triborough Bridge (125th Street).

To Brooklyn: Brooklyn Bridge (near City Hall), Manhattan Bridge (Forsyth Street), Williamsburg Bridge (Delancey Street), Brooklyn-Battery Tunnel (at S tip of Manhattan).

Staten Island: ferry from Battery Park, Verrazano-Narrows Bridge from Fort Hamilton Parkway in Brooklyn.

Culture

New York is the cultural centre of the United States, with the country's largest concentration of theatres (some 40 on and around Broadway and 250 little theatres), a number of leading museums, two opera-houses, several major orchestras, over a dozen ballet and dance companies and the second largest library in the United States, the New York Public Library.

Here, too, are the headquarters of most US publishing houses and of almost all the leading periodicals. There are large numbers of bookshops and antiquarian booksellers; and the Public Library is backed up by a whole range of smaller libraries catering for special interests. The most respected US newspaper, the "New York Times", is published here, and the country's five main television channels are based in New York.

Universities and colleges

New York has more than 50 universities and colleges, the great majority of them in Manhattan. The oldest and perhaps the most renowned is Columbia University, founded in 1754 as King's College; the largest New York University, founded in 1831, which has over 30,000 students. Others are the Rockefeller University, which has a mainly scientific orientation, the Roman Catholic Fordham University and the New School of Social Research, which achieved some prominence in the 1930s as the "University in Exile". New York also has six medical schools, three major academies of music, numerous drama schools and a number of art schools. All these institutions are privately run. There is also the City University, with 18 colleges in New York City, which was founded in 1849 as the City College, the first higher educational establishment in the United States to charge no fees.

Bird's-eye view of Columbia University and East Harlem

New York holds unchallenged supremacy in the United States as a centre of the performing arts. There are something like 1000 premières in New York theatres every year, and during the winter months there are between 120 and 150 musical events every week. A special place in the musical world is occupied by the Metropolitan Opera, one of the world's most renowned opera-houses, which puts on spectacular productions by both American and foreign companies. All the leading American and many European orchestras perform every year in New York, supplementing the four weekly concerts of the New York Philharmonic Orchestra, which has played a leading part in New York's musical life since 1842.

Drama, opera, music

With 20 art museums and as many more devoted to science, history and other fields, some 400 galleries and a variety of cultural bodies from many European, Asian and African countries, the New York art scene is rich and varied, covering the whole range from traditional to avant-garde art.

The arts

Art also finds expression in New York in the form of mural paintings on the outsides of buildings and works of modern sculpture set up in the open air (see A to Z, Sculpture).

Commerce and Industry

In spite of the many problems of the past decade – an exodus of population and of large firms, financial crises, shortage of

New York, centre of world trade

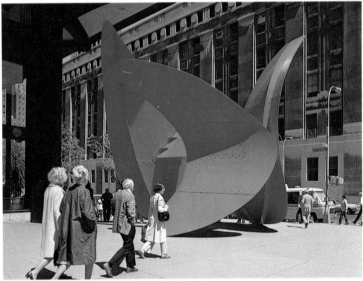

A "stabile" by Alexander Calder, World Trade Center

housing, increased crime – New York has retained its economic predominance in the United States and is now the world's largest capital market and its chief financial centre. The New York Stock Exchange still sets the pace for the world's markets, and the fear that it would abandon the Wall Street area and move over to New Jersey has been dispelled. And in addition to the New York Exchange there are the American Stock Exchange and numerous commodity exchanges.

At the end of the 1960s 140 out of the 500 largest firms in the United States had their headquarters in New York. The figure has now fallen to below 100, since it is in this field that the move out to the suburbs has been most marked.

Six of the country's seven largest banks, with total assets of almost 200,000 million dollars (Citicorp, Chase Manhattan Bank, Manufacturers Hanover Trust, Morgan Guaranty Trust, Chemical Bank and Bankers Trust), are based in New York, as are three of the five largest life insurance corporations (Metropolitan Life, Equitable Life and New York Life); and a third of the country's largest retail firms and almost 17% of wholesalers have their head office in the city.

Regional industries

The industry of greatest importance to New York's economy is textiles, in which around a quarter of a million people are employed. Second and third places are taken by the graphic trades and the foodstuffs industries. All other industries together employ fewer people than the "big three". Of major importance are the construction industries, although these are very sensitive to changing economic conditions and show greater fluctuations in numbers employed than other branches of industry.

New York has a number of large department stores, including Macy's, Gimbel's, Bloomingdale's, Abraham and Straus, Lord and Taylor, Saks Fifth Avenue and Bergdorf Goodman which are trend-setters, particularly in the fashion trade. The total number of retail shops is legion, selling every conceivable variety of goods. It is not surprising that New York enjoys the reputation of being the best – and in many fields the cheapest – shopping centre in the world.

Retail trade

New York is without equal in the United States as a centre of the various service industries such as market research, advertising – which has become synonymous with Madison Avenue – public relations, management consultancy, stock-broking and architectural design, which all flourish here.

Service trades and tourism

Some 15,000 restaurants and hundreds of hotels with a total of over 100,000 rooms cater for the needs of the 17 million visitors, including 2 million from outside the United States, who come to New York every year. The number of congresses and conferences held in New York is increasing all the time, and will take another leap forward when the huge new congress centre now under construction on the banks of the Hudson between 42nd and 46th Streets is completed.

Finally New York has more lawyers and doctors than any other American city, both proportionately and in absolute terms.

In 1975 New York was involved in a financial crisis which brought it within sight of bankruptcy, and was able to meet its obligations only with the assistance of New York State and the federal government and at the price of sacrificing some of its previous budgetary independence and accepting a measure of outside control. Within a few years the number of municipal employees fell by 20%, whereupon the reduction in police strength was reflected in increased crime and the cutting-down of the cleansing services in dirtier streets. Fares were increased on public transport but the standard of service continued to decline. By the end of 1981, however, the economy had strengthened and New York City was able to maintain a virtually balanced budget. This improvement shows every sign of continuing.

Problems of a great city

Notable New Yorkers

John Jacob Astor, one of the first great American entrepreneurs, came to New York from his native village of Walldorf near Heidelberg in SW Germany at the age of 20. After some time as a dealer in musical instruments he moved into the fur trade, and in 1808 established the American Fur Company. This was followed by two other companies, and he secured almost a monopoly of the American fur trade. Most of his enormous wealth, however, came from speculation in real estate, in the course of which he acquired a great deal of property, particularly in Manhattan. When he died his fortune was estimated at 25 million dollars, making him the richest man in

John Jacob Astor
(1763–1848)

America. Shortly before his death he gave 400,000 dollars for the building of the Astor Library, America's first public library.

Lyonel Feininger
(1871–1956)

Born in New York – his parents were both musicians – the painter and graphic artist Lyonel Feininger spent 50 years of his life (1887–1937) in Europe, mainly in Germany, where he at first worked as a caricaturist and illustrator and then, in 1907, began to paint. He was friendly with Franz Marc, Kandinsky, Klee and Jawlensky, and from 1919 to 1933 taught at the Bauhaus in Dessau. In 1937 he returned to New York, where he received a number of commissions for the 1939 World's Fair. His work is characterised by interpenetrating planes of prismatic colour and striking light effects. He became best known for his townscapes and seascapes.

Robert Fulton
(1765–1815)

A native of Pennsylvania, Robert Fulton began his career as a painter but later became an engineer; during the 20 years he spent in London and Paris (1786–1805) he produced a series of inventions, including a submarine and torpedoes, in which he failed to interest either the British or the French. Returning to New York, he built the "Clermont", the first steamship, which in 1807 sailed from New York up the Hudson to Albany and back in 62 hours. Shortly before his death he built the first steam-propelled warship, which was never tried out.

George Gershwin
(1898–1937)

George Gershwin, creator of a distinctively American form of serious music, was a native of Brooklyn who began his musical career as song plugger from a music publishing firm. He published his first song at the age of 18, and gained his first great success three years later with "Swanee". During the twenties he achieved fame with his "Rhapsody in Blue", a symphonic jazz composition, his "Piano Concerto in F Major" and a number of musicals written in collaboration with his brother Ira. His political satire "Of Thee I Sing" won him the Pulitzer Prize in 1931. His most mature work, and his last, was the opera "Porgy and Bess", written in 1935. Two years later he died of a brain tumour. As the first composer to make jazz rhythms acceptable in "serious" music his reputation is secure.

Alexander Hamilton
(1755–1804)

Alexander Hamilton, one of the fathers of the American constitution, came to New York from the West Indian island of Nevis in 1773. At the beginning of the War of American Independence he mustered a troop of artillery and attracted the attention of George Washington, whose confidential secretary he became in 1777. During the war he distinguished himself in a number of engagements.
At the 1787 constitutional convention he favoured a strongly centralised union. As first Secretary of the Treasury (1789–95) he brought order into the country's finances, which had been shattered by the war, on the basis of a new fiscal system. Strongly conservative, he opposed Jefferson's democratic programme and advocated an authoritarian state.
Hamilton died after being wounded in a duel with Aaron Burr, the Democratic presidential candidate.

O. Henry
(1862–1910)

O. Henry (real name William Sidney Porter) was the first great master of the short story. Sentenced to five years in prison for misappropriation of funds in a bank in which he was employed, he wrote his first stories in prison and soon became famous. In

Robert Fulton

O. Henry

Theodore Roosevelt

1900 he went to New York, finding an abundance of material for his stories in the people and the life of the great city.
Almost all of his 600 stories are written to the same pattern, with a surprise twist at the end. He did not live long to enjoy his fame, dying of tuberculosis in 1910.

The painter and graphic artist Edward Hopper, who had a studio in Washington Square for many years, was over 50 before the first retrospective exhibition of his work was held in a New York museum. He was unequalled as a portrayer of the life of New York, the activity of its streets and the loneliness of man in the city.
He left more than 2000 oil paintings, watercolours, drawings, sketches and prints to the Whitney Museum of American Art, which organised the first comprehensive exhibition of his work in 1980.

Edward Hopper (1882–1967)

Washington Irving began his working life as a lawyer and spent some time as a diplomat before becoming the first American writer to achieve a reputation outside the United States. His first work was published in 1802, and with the appearance of his burlesque "Diedrich Knickerbocker's History of New York" in 1809 he became the accepted chronicler of his native city. He spent the years 1804–6 and 1815–32 in Europe, and from 1842 to 1845 was American ambassador in Madrid. In addition to his tales and various historical works he wrote a five-volume life of George Washington during the last five years of his own life.

Washington Irving (1783–1859)

Henry James, brother of the philosopher William James, ranks as one of America's leading novelists, though he spent the last 40 years of his life in London and acquired British citizenship in 1915. The themes of his works were supplied by his own experiences in two continents. Written in a very characteristic convoluted style, they depict the encounter between the men and women of the New World and the traditions and conventions of Europe. James wrote more than a dozen novels and over a hundred short stories. In his early work he shows himself to be a skilled portrayer of life in New York. A complete edition of his works published in 1961–4 runs to 26 volumes, plus four volumes of autobiographical writings.

Henry James (1843–1916)

19

Notable New Yorkers

Henry Miller
(1891–1980)

Henry Miller earned more headlines than any other American writer of the 20th c. with works which were decried and banned by some as pornography and celebrated as masterpieces by others. After leaving school early, Miller became a casual worker before beginning to write in the mid twenties. From 1930 to 1940 he lived mainly in Paris, where he wrote his well known novels "Tropic of Cancer" and "Tropic of Capricorn". His novels and stories, containing a strong autobiographical element, were directed against the Puritan taboos of American society. In his trilogy of novels, "Sexus", "Plexus" and "Nexus", he made sexuality his literary theme.

John Pierpont Morgan
(1837–1913)

After a brief period as a student at Göttingen University, John Pierpont Morgan returned to the United States and arrived in New York at the age of 20. In 1860 he founded the firm of J. P. Morgan and Co., which acted as an agent of his father's banking house in London. Founding his own banking house in 1895, he acquired great influence on railway development in the United States, and in 1901 played a major part in the establishment of the United States Steel Corporation, which developed into the largest steel trust in the United States. In addition he was perhaps the largest private collector of art, manuscripts and books of his day. Most of his pictures are now in the Metropolitan Museum of Art; his other treasures can be seen in the Pierpont Morgan Library which he built in New York.

Adolph S. Ochs
(1858–1935)

The newspaper publisher Adolph S. Ochs, born in Knoxville, Tennessee, the son of a German Jewish immigrant, began his career at the age of 11 as a newspaper-boy in his native town and later became an apprentice printer. In 1875 he went to Chattanooga, Tennessee. Three years later, at the age of 20, he bought the local paper, the "Chattanooga Times", and within four years had made it one of the leading newspapers of the southern states.

Ochs's great coup came in 1896, when he paid 75,000 dollars for the "New York Times", an old-established paper which was in difficulties in the intensely competitive New York newspaper world. By the time of his retirement in 1933 Ochs had built it up into America's leading daily, with the slogan "All the news that's fit to print".

The "New York Times", now a limited company, has grown into a large concern with wide interests in publishing, papermaking, periodicals, radio and television, but it is still directed by Ochs's descendants: the present head of the firm is his grandson, Arthur Ochs Sulzberger.

Eugene O'Neill
(1888–1953)

Eugene O'Neill, the leading US dramatist, spent his early years in New York. Having contracted tuberculosis, he spent some time in a sanatorium, where, at the age of 24, he began to read plays, being particularly influenced by the work of Ibsen and Strindberg. His first one-act play was performed by the Provincetown Players in New York. He received the Pulitzer Prize in 1920 for his first full-length play "Beyond the Horizon", and three further Pulitzers for "Anna Christie" (1922), "Strange Interlude" (1928) and "Long Day's Journey into Night" (1956, posthumously). He was awarded the Nobel Prize in 1936.

Theodore Roosevelt, 26th President of the United States (1901–9), is the only President to have been born in New York. He came from a Dutch family which had settled in New York (then called Nieuw (New) Amsterdam) in the middle of the 17th c. After studying law at Harvard and Columbia University he stood for election as Mayor of New York at the age of 28 but was defeated by his Democratic opponent. In 1895 he became president of the New York City Police Commissioners, in 1898 governor of New York State and in 1900 Vice-President of the United States. After President McKinley's murder in September 1901 he became President at the age of 42 – the youngest President ever. He was re-elected in 1904, and in the following year he mediated between Russia and Japan and brought the Russo-Japanese War to an end, for which he was awarded the Nobel Peace Prize.

In 1908 he secured the election of William H. Taft as his successor, but when Taft proved too conservative for his taste he founded the Progressive party, with himself as presidential candidate at the 1912 election. The result was to split the Republican vote and bring about the election of a Democrat, Woodrow Wilson.

Roosevelt also made a name for himself as a natural scientist and hunter. A river in Brazil which he discovered is named after him.

Theodore Roosevelt (1858–1919)

The politician and publicist Carl Schurz, perhaps the most prominent of the Germans who emigrated to the United States after the suppression of the German revolution of 1848, became a newspaper publisher, general, senator, diplomat and finally Secretary of the Interior under President Grant

Carl Schurz (1829–1906)

Washington Irving

Carl Schurz

(1877–91). True to his liberal principles, he sought to achieve better treatment of negroes and Indians and fought against any excesses directed against these population groups. He was also concerned to maintain the interests of German Americans. He is commemorated by the Carl Schurz Park on East River (86th Street) and a monument by the Austrian sculptor, Karl Bitter, in Morningside Park.

Walt Whitman (1819–92)

Walt Whitman, the first American lyric poet to achieve world fame, came from a Quaker family. He left school with only a primary education but made up for this by private study. Until the age of 25 he worked as a journeyman printer, journalist and school-teacher; then in 1846 he became editor of the "Brooklyn Daily Eagle", but lost this job after only two years on account of his anti-slavery sentiments.

In 1855 he published the first edition of his most famous work, "Leaves of Grass", of which there were eight further editions during his lifetime. During the 1860s his works both in verse and prose reflected the experience of the Civil War, during which he devoted himself to visiting the wounded.

In 1873 Whitman suffered a stroke which condemned him to relative inactivity for the rest of his life.

The vigorous rhythms of his blank verse, the self-assurance of his manner and the unity of the body and of nature which he proclaimed, influenced the poetry of the 20th c., and the exuberance of his hymns was seen as an expression of the American spirit and of democracy, as the poetry of a new age.

History of New York

1524

The Italian navigator Giovanni da Verrazano sails into New York Bay and sights Manhattan – the first European to do so. He surveys the E coast of America on behalf of King Francis I of France and claims the whole territory for the French crown. But since France is at war with Spain the new colony attracts no interest.

1609

An Englishman, Henry Hudson, becomes the first European to set foot on the soil of New York. (He had been commissioned by the Dutch East India Company to find the North-West Passage to China and Japan, for the discovery of which the Dutch government had offered a prize of 25,000 guilders.) Hudson sails W across the Atlantic, reconnoitres the American coast from Maine to Virginia, then returns N and sails into New York Bay and up the river which still bears his name, hoping to find a route to the Pacific.

Recognising his error, he returns down the Hudson, makes several landings on Manhattan and then sails back to Europe.

The first governor of a number of small Dutch settlements on the banks of the Hudson and the S end of Manhattan, Peter Minnewit of Wesel on the lower Rhine, buys the island from the Manna-hatta Indians for only 60 guilders and names the settlement Nieuw Amsterdam (New Amsterdam). The establishment of the Dutch East India Company promotes the development of trade, including trade with the Indians.	1626
Foundation of Breuckelen (Brooklyn).	1646
Peter Stuyvesant is appointed governor. He soon develops into a dictator, suppresses political opposition, abolishes freedom of worship and attempts to prevent the immigration of Jews and Protestants.	1647
New Amsterdam has a population of barely 1000.	1650
Stuyvesant has a wall built from the Hudson to East River, along the line of present-day Wall Street, as a protection against British attacks.	1653
During the second Anglo-Dutch war (1664/65–7) New Amsterdam is taken by a British fleet without a shot being fired. The settlement is renamed New York and becomes the property of the Duke of York, Charles II's brother.	1664
The Dutch retake New York and change its name to Nieuw Orange (New Orange).	1673
The Dutch are driven out by British forces.	1674
The result of a legal suit by the colonial governor against the publisher of the first opposition newspaper, the "New York Weekly Journal", is to establish the freedom of the press in America.	1735
Outbreak of the War of American Independence. New York has a population of 25,000. Its port handles a bigger trade than Boston or Philadelphia.	1776
George Washington, leader of the rebellious colonies, moves his headquarters from Boston to New York, but loses the battle of Long Island and is compelled to leave the British in occupation until the end of the war.	April 1776
The Continental Congress carries a motion for the independence of the 13 states on the E coast of America. Two days later the Declaration of Independence is adopted.	2 July 1776
British troops surrender at Yorktown.	19 October 1781
Treaty of Paris: Britain recognises the independence of its former American colonies. During the long period of British occupation New York has been plundered and partly destroyed by fire and the population has been decimated.	1783

History of New York

1784	The first meeting of New York State legislature is held in the city (which remains capital of the state until superseded by Albany in 1797).
1789	New York briefly becomes capital of the young nation and seat of the Union government (a role it loses to Philadelphia in the following year). George Washington is sworn in as first President of the United States in Federal Hall. The population of New York is now over 30,000.
1820	With a population of over 150,000, New York displaces Pennsylvania as the largest city in the country, in spite of epidemics of cholera and yellow fever, a series of fires and civil disturbances.
1825	After the opening of the Erie Canal the first ship from Buffalo sails down the Hudson to New York. The city's predominance is enhanced by this new route to the W.
1848 onwards	After the repression of the 1848 revolutions in Europe there is an influx of political refugees and other immigrants, bringing the population over the half-million mark.
1853	First New York International Exposition in the newly built Crystal Palace.
1861–5	Eleven southern states secede from the Union over the slavery question and form a separate Confederation. The Civil War ends, after much loss of life, in the victory of the northern states. After the war many negroes come to New York from the southern states.
1869	Central Park (at this time lying on the northern outskirts of the city) is opened.
1870	The population passes the million mark. The revelation of large-scale corruption in the city administration, involving the misappropriation of 75 million dollars, does not destroy the city's creditworthiness.
1882	Continuing influx of immigrants. The number of Germans coming in reaches the record figure of a quarter of a million, some 200,000 of whom remain in New York.
1883	Opening of the Metropolitan Opera House and Brooklyn Bridge.
1886	Erection of the Statue of Liberty.
1898	Establishment of Greater New York by the amalgamation of New York (Manhattan) with the counties of Kings (Brooklyn), Bronx, Queens and Staten Island. With a population of almost 3·5 million, New York is now the largest city in the world after London.
1900	First Automobile Show held in Madison Square Garden.

1626: Peter Minnewit buys Manhattan from the Indians

1783: American troops enter New York

History of New York

1904	First subway line opened (City Hall to Times Square). Times Square becomes the first square lit by electricity.
1913	The population of Greater New York passes the 5 million mark. Manhattan, with almost 2·4 million inhabitants, reaches its highest population. (By 1980 it has fallen by over a million.) Completion of the Woolworth Building, the highest building in the world until 1931.
October 1929	The Wall Street crash on "Black Friday" marks the beginning of a world economic crisis which lasts almost ten years.
1931	William F. Lamb builds the Empire State Building, for 40 years the highest in the world (381 m – 1250 ft). Also constructed at this time are the Chrysler Building, the RCA Building and the George Washington Bridge over the Hudson.
1932	Opening of Radio City Music Hall.
1939–40	New York's second World's Fair, held in Flushing (Queens). Opening of the LaGuardia Airport, named after Fiorello LaGuardia, Mayor of New York.
1952	The United Nations move into their new headquarters on East River from their temporary home in a converted factory on the outskirts of the city.
1960	Two aircraft collide over New York, with 134 deaths.
1962	An aircraft crashes soon after take-off from Idlewild (now J. F. Kennedy) Airport, with 95 deaths.
8–9 November 1965	In the year of the third New York World's Fair the city is paralysed for 16 hours by the failure of the power supply. Soon afterwards life in New York is brought to a standstill again by a ten-day strike of subway and bus staffs.
1970	The completion of its N tower (420 m – 1380 ft) makes the World Trade Center briefly the world's highest building (soon to be superseded by the Sears Tower in Chicago).
1975	New York City faces bankruptcy, but is saved from total collapse by a bridging loan from the federal government, accompanied by the establishment of a control agency to watch over municipal finances and a reduction in the number of municipal employees.
July 1977	New York suffers a further breakdown in the power supply, this time lasting 27 hours.
April 1980	There is a further strike by subway and bus staffs, lasting 14 days.

The building of new luxury hotels and large skyscrapers points to the city's gradual recovery from economic stagnation. There is a fall in the number of unemployed; a recovery is in progress. On the other hand crime increases; public transport is worse than ever and the rehabilitation of slum areas makes only slow progress.

1981

In spite of the poor state of the economy, the continued erection of skyscraper office blocks is seen as a sign of confidence in the future by the business world.

1982

This year sees more skyscrapers finished than ever before. The city's financial problems seem finally to have been overcome.

1983

Quotations

"Fifth Avenue is a street where a lot of people spend money on buying things they don't need in order to impress people they don't like."

Anonymous

"I shall never encompass New York in words. I no longer seek to encompass this city: I become dissolved in it. Words, pictures, knowledge, expectations are of no service: it is pointless to establish whether they are true or false. There is no confrontation possible with the things to be encountered in New York. They exist in a fashion all their own: they are *there*. And I gaze and gaze, astonished as a blind man must be who has recovered his sight."
("L'Amérique au jour le jour")

Simone de Beauvoir
(b. 1908)

"New York is a myth, and much more than that – a demon, a sphinx, a crater, a Moloch, an idol, a hell, a snakepit, an excrement, a volcano and much else besides. Writers and journalists, painters and photographers have repeatedly tried to uncover this myth and reveal the reality behind it; but this can never be more than partially achieved, for everything that is said about this city is right and at the same time wrong. For every theory there is a proof, there is a proof for every assertion . . . New York is myth and reality at the same time, and you are continually tempted to compare the images that emerge from the subconscious with what you see in front of you: to compare and sometimes to confuse . . .

"A city of stone and of human faces, a city that lives in the permanent and in the transient . . . When the theatres come out and people stream to the taxi-ranks and the subway each face has its individual stamp, each face tells a different story, contains a different secret . . .

"In these faces I have tried to understand this country – its history and its present, and sometimes too its future."

Horst Bienek
(b. 1930)

"The tone of the best society in this city is like that of Boston; here and there, it may be, with a greater infusion of the mercantile spirit, but generally polished and refined, and always most hospitable. The houses and tables are elegant; the

Charles Dickens
(1812–70)

27

hours later and more rakish; and there is, perhaps, a greater spirit of contention in reference to appearances, and the display of wealth and costly living. The ladies are singularly beautiful."
("American Notes")

Gustav Frenssen
(1863–1945)

"I am staying in the largest hotel in the world. I take the express lift up to my room on the 17th floor, from which I have a wide view over the Hudson; far below me are houses and churches. They want to hear that it all makes a powerful impression on me; but it does not. It does not strike me with astonishment, and I feel not the slightest inclination to admire what I see. I am not a man who measures greatness with a yardstick: my scale of measurement is beauty. And so the greatest things I have seen have been the clouds which lowered over the Hudson yesterday and a pretty girl who walked across the lobby with a splendidly lively gait. They know how to walk here, I can tell you: here every limb, every muscle is in play. It is strange that in an old country like Europe we should have to re-learn the art of walking; but you will see, we shall learn it . . . from these American girls."
("Letters from America")

O. Henry
(1862–1910)

"Bagdad-on-the-Subway."

Le Corbusier
(1887–1965)

"New York is a vertical city which bears the mark of the new age. It is a catastrophe which an unkind fate has brought down on a courageous and confident people, but a grandiose and magnificent catastrophe."
("Quand les cathédrales étaient blanches")

Vladimir Mayakovsky
(1893–1930)

"I love New York on weekdays in autumn and on working days. "At six in the morning storm and rain. And cloud – cloud that will last until midday.
"We are overwhelmed with electric light. The huge bulk of the buildings and the movement of the traffic seem multiplied tenfold in the mirror into which rain has converted the asphalt. In the narrow spaces between the buildings the wind, now a hurricane, howls like a trumpet blast. It tears the placards off the walls and tries to blow the passers-by off their feet. It rages with impunity along the streets which stretch for miles from end to end of Manhattan and, far away, hurls itself into the ocean . . . "Out there, in the hours before dawn, there passes the dark purple mass of the negroes who are given all the hardest and dirtiest work. Later, around 7 o'clock, the human flood is entirely white. Hundreds of thousands of men and women are hurrying to their work. At this hour there are still no automobiles or even taxis to be seen . . .
"New York feels at its best in the morning and during a thunderstorm, when no idlers or superfluous people are to be seen on the streets – only members of the great army of workers who live in this city of ten million people."
("My Journey to America")

Paul Morand
(1888–1976)

"New York is not America, but it is easy to see that the whole of America would like to be New York."

Viktor Nekrasov
(b. 1911)

"On the summit of the Empire State Building is an observation platform. When you stand up there, with the wind blowing round you, and look down on this giant of a city, this octopus of a city – call it what you will – you cannot but feel excitement. Huddled together far below are the skyscrapers, and between them are what appear to be swarms of ants and a thousand tiny toy cars. There are East River and Brooklyn Bridge . . . and there the Hudson with its piers and its shipping . . . The only place where I have had a similar feeling was on the summit of Mount Elbruz. The Caucasus at your feet and the whole world below you! There you are overwhelmed by the grandeur and beauty of nature, here by the grandeur and beauty of man; for all this he has made – made it with his brain and his hands."

"New York appears to me as infinitely more American than Boston, Chicago, or Washington. It has no peculiar attribute of its own, as have those three cities, Boston in its literature and accomplished intelligence, Chicago in its internal trade, and Washington in its congressional and State politics. New York has its literary aspirations, its commercial grandeur, and – heaven knows – it has its politics also. But these do not strike the visitor as being specially characteristic of the city. That it is pre-eminently American is its glory or its disgrace, as men of different ways of thinking may decide upon it. Free institutions, general education, and the ascendancy of dollars are the words written on every paving-stone along Fifth Avenue, down Broadway, and up Wall Street."
("North America", 1862)

Anthony Trollope
(1815–82)

"To tell the story of New York would be to write a social history of the world."

H. G. Wells
(1866–1946)

New York from A to Z

**American Museum of Natural History and Hayden Planetarium

C/D4

Situation
Central Park West and 79th Street

Subway station
81st Street (lines AA, B, CC)

Buses
10, 17

Opening times
Mon., Tues., Thurs., Sun.
10 a.m.–5.45 p.m., Wed.,
Fri., Sat. 10 a.m.–9 p.m.

The American Museum of Natural History, founded in 1869, is New York's oldest museum. With considerable extensions to the original buildings, it is now one of the largest museums of its kind in the United States.

First floor
The first floor (in British terms the ground floor) is mainly devoted to the natural history of the North American continent, with its flora and fauna and its indigenous inhabitants (Eskimos and Indians) presented in lifelike groups.

Second floor
On this floor are major exhibits illustrating the natural and cultural history of black Africa.

Third floor
Birds of North America; reptiles and amphibians; life of the Indians; African mammals.

Fourth floor
History of the Earth; early and late mammals; numerous dinosaurs of the earlier and later periods, with skeletons and reconstructions, and fossil fishes; Library and Library Gallery.

American Museum of Natural History

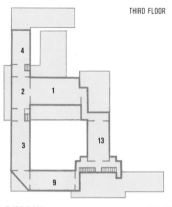

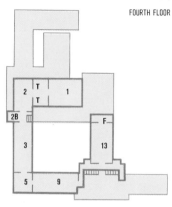

THIRD FLOOR
1 North American birds
2 Primates
3 Gallery 3
4 Indians of the eastern woodlands
  and plains

9 Reptiles and amphibians
13 African mammals
FOURTH FLOOR
1 Library
2 History of the Earth
2B Library Gallery

3 Late mammals
5 Early mammals
9 Late dinosaurs
13 Early dinosaurs
F Fossil fishes
T Toilets

American Museum of Natural History

FIRST FLOOR
1 Indians of the NW coast
1A Gallery 77
2 77th Street Foyer
2A Molluscs and man
2B Museum shop
3 Man and nature
4 Biology of man
5 North American forests
7 Auditorium
7A Eskimos
7B Small mammals
8 Minerals and precious stones

9 Biology of the invertebrates
10 Life in the ocean; biology of
   fishes
11 Education Hall
11A Education Gallery
12 Theodore Roosevelt Memorial
13 North American mammals
18 Planetarium
19 Biology of birds
D Discovery Room
P Car park
T Toilets

SECOND FLOOR
A People Center
B Calder Laboratory
C Center Gallery
D Natural Science Center
1 Man in Africa
2 Birds of the world
4 Mexico and Central America
7 Akeley Gallery
12 Theodore Roosevelt Memorial
13 African mammals
19 Oceanic birds
T Toilets

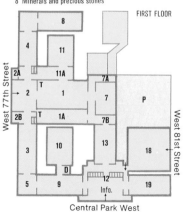

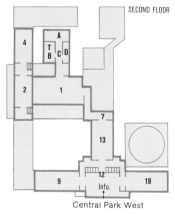

Other activities
The Museum has its own research laboratories and sends out expeditions to all parts of the world. It also publishes a monthly journal, "Natural History", which has a large circulation, and it puts on many special exhibitions every year.

Hayden Planetarium

Within the Museum is the Hayden Planetarium, which can be visited separately. It has excellent explanatory displays illustrating phenomena in the atmosphere and in space, with a model of the solar system, a reproduction of the surface of the moon, a meteorite weighing 34 tons and a Zeiss VI projector installed in 1969. There are special presentations in the Guggenheim Space Theater, and in adjoining galleries are exhibits illustrating the history of astronomy.

Asia House Gallery   E5

Situation
Park Avenue and 70th Street

Subway station
68th Street (line 6)

Buses
1, 2, 3, 4

Opening times
Tues.–Sat. 10 a.m.–5 p.m.,
Thurs. until 8.30 p.m., Sun.
noon–5 p.m.

The Asia Society was founded in 1956 by John D. Rockefeller III, but soon outgrew its original premises at 112 East 64th Street, a fine building designed by Philip Johnson which is now occupied by the Russell Sage Foundation. The Society's new home was opened in April 1981 after a building period of two years.

Here are displayed the Society's fine collection of sculpture, porcelain and painting from China, Japan, India and South-East Asia; but its interests also extend into the fields of music, cinema and other aspects of Asian culture. The Society regularly mounts special exhibitions of Asian art.
There are branches of the Society in Washington and Houston.

El Barrio   E1/2

Subway station
116th Street (line 6)

Bus
102

El Barrio is the name given to an area in East Harlem occupied mainly by Puerto Ricans and other Spanish-speaking population groups who have come to New York in recent years from the Caribbean area and from Central and South America. The boundaries of the area, which is steadily expanding, are not exactly defined; but broadly it lies to the E of Fifth Avenue between 103rd Street and 125th Street (which is one of the main streets of Harlem). This part of the town is estimated to have more burnt-out, vandalised and unoccupied houses than any other area in New York except the southern Bronx, but nevertheless has a population of something like 200,000.

This is a district which most visitors will fight shy of, for it is one of New York's worst slum areas, and its rehabilitation is likely to be a lengthy process. One feature of potential interest is the Marqueta, a market held under the railway viaduct (Park Avenue, 110th–115th Streets), where good bargains can sometimes be obtained.

On the Bowery

Bowery E9/F10

The Bowery, New York's second oldest street (after Broadway), has a bad reputation as the haunt of alcoholic dropouts ("bums"). In fact the Bowery, one of the widest streets in the city, running for exactly a mile from Catham Square in Chinatown to Cooper Square, is much better than its reputation. It is perfectly safe to visit the Bowery provided you do not take photographs or otherwise draw attention to yourself: the worst that is likely to happen to you is to be pestered for money. In addition to the hostels for alcoholics run by the Salvation Army and other charitable organisations, there are numerous shops, theatres, rock clubs, etc., and artists and writers live in the apartment blocks, many of them very much down at heel – the kind of mixture that can perhaps be found only in New York.

Subway station
Astor Place (line 6)

Bowne House

This house, built in 1661 by John Bowne, a Quaker, is the oldest building within the city limits. The furniture and furnishings date mostly from the 17th and 18th c. The kitchen with its huge chimney has been preserved almost exactly as it was more than 300 years ago.
Bowne House is open to the public on Tuesdays, Saturdays and Sundays from 2.30 to 4.30 p.m.

Address
37–01 Bowne Street,
Flushing (Queens)

Subway station
Main Street (line 7)

*Bronx Zoo

Situation
Southern Boulevard and
185th Street (Bronx)

Subway stations
East Tremont Avenue and
Boston Road (lines 2 and 5)

Opening times
Daily 10 a.m.–5 p.m., Sun.
and public holidays 10 a.m.–
5.30 p.m.; Nov.–Jan., daily
10 a.m.–4.30 p.m.

Admission free
Tues., Wed. and Thurs.

Officially the New York Zoological Park but known to New Yorkers only as the Bronx Zoo, this is the largest of New York's five zoos, with an area of 100 ha (250 acres). (The other four are in Central Park (see entry), Manhattan; Prospect Park, Brooklyn; Flushing Meadows, Queens; and Barrett Park, Staten Island.)

The Bronx Zoo – which, like the New York Botanical Garden (see entry), is part of Bronx Park – was originally laid out in 1899, but a programme of reconstruction carried out in recent years and not yet complete has largely transformed it. The old cages have been almost all replaced by open enclosures, in which the animals live in surroundings as similar as possible to their natural habitat. There are also many modern houses for birds, monkeys, beasts of prey, waterfowl, reptiles, penguins and gorillas.

A particuarly interesting feature is the arrangement of the enclosures according to the continents from which the animals come.

*Brooklyn Botanic Garden

Address
1000 Washington Avenue
(Brooklyn)

Subway station
Eastern Parkway/Brooklyn
Museum (lines 2 and 3)

Buses
Prospect Park (lines D, M
and B)

This botanic garden, easily reached from Manhattan, has steadily grown more attractive over the 70 years of its existence. Within its 20 ha (50 acres) it contains more than 12,000 different species of plants, including 900 kinds of roses alone, presenting a glorious spectacle during their summer flowering period. There is also a beautiful avenue of Japanese cherry-trees, seen at their best at the end of April and beginning of May.

In winter the glasshouses are a particular attraction.

A visit to the Botanic Garden can conveniently be combined with a visit to the Brooklyn Museum (see entry).

There is no charge for admission.

Opening times are: Tues.–Fri. 8 a.m.–6 p.m.; at weekends and holidays 10 a.m.–6 p.m.

*Brooklyn Bridge   F11

Subway station
Brooklyn Bridge (lines 4, 5
and 6)

New York has no fewer than 65 bridges, 18 of them linking Manhattan with the other boroughs and with New Jersey.

The Brooklyn Bridge spans the East River, linking Manhattan with Brooklyn. This suspension bridge, 500 m (1595 ft) long between the two pylons, was built in 1883 by the German-American engineer John A. Roebling and his son Washington A. Roebling.

Brooklyn Bridge

Brooklyn Children's Museum

Brooklyn Children's Museum, founded in 1899, aims to give children an understanding of the various aspects of technology, ethnology and natural history in the most vivid and interesting way. Altogether it has more than 40,000 exhibits, including working models which enable children to learn about many fields of knowledge in practical fashion.

The museum also has a large collection of dolls, rocks and fossils, shells, costumes and African artefacts.

There is a charge for admission.

Brooklyn
145 Brooklyn Avenue
(Brooklyn)

Subway stations
Kingston Avenue (line 2),
Kingston/Throop (line A)

Opening times
Wed.–Mon. 1–5 p.m.

*Brooklyn Museum

Were it not that the Brooklyn Museum lies rather off the usual tourist track, it would be one of the most visited museums in New York. Its departments of Egyptian, Near Eastern and Oriental art rank among the finest collections of the kind to be seen in the city. It can be reached by subway from Manhattan in half an hour.

The building was originally erected in 1897 but has undergone much subsequent alteration, not always to its advantage. Thus the flight of steps leading up to the second floor (in British terms first floor) has been removed, leaving the museum with a very unimpressive ground-floor entrance.

Address
188 Eastern Parkway

Subway station
Eastern Parkway (line 4 or 5 to Nevins Street, then change to 2 or 3)

Opening times
Wed.–Sat. 10 a.m.–5 p.m.,
Sun. noon–5 p.m., public
holidays 1–5 p.m.

Brooklyn Museum

Brooklyn Museum

Closed
Mon. and Tues.

First floor (ground floor)

Primitive arts (from Africa, the South Seas, American Indians and pre-Columbian peoples); special exhibitions.

Second floor

Mainly devoted to the art of China, Japan, Thailand, India and Persia.

Third floor

Coptic, Egyptian, Greek, Roman and Near Eastern cultures; Wilbour Library of Egyptology.

Fourth floor

European and American costume; 25 completely furnished American rooms (1715–1880); a Brooklyn house of the Dutch colonial period (1675), transported here from its original site; silver and pewter, china, glass and furniture from the early days of America.

Fifth floor

European and American painting and sculpture. The collection of American art is particularly extensive.

A visit to the Museum can conveniently be combined with a visit to the adjoining Brooklyn Botanic Gardens (see entry).

Castle Clinton National Monument   E12

Castle Clinton has had many vicissitudes in the course of its history. It was built before the 1812 war with Britain, but had only a short military career: after serving for some years as the headquarters of the 3rd Military District it was converted in 1824 into a place of entertainment (fireworks, brass band concerts, etc.). Twenty years later it was roofed over and became a concert hall, in which the famous "Swedish nightingale", Jenny Lind, sang before an audience of 6000 in 1850.

From 1855 Castle Clinton was used as a depot for immigrants, and from 1896 to 1941 it housed a popular aquarium. Thereafter it was unoccupied for 34 years and lost its roof and upper floor; then in 1975 after extensive restoration work it was reopened as a national monument.

Admission is free.

Situation
Battery Park

Subway stations
Bowling Green (lines 4 and 5), South Ferry (line 1), Whitehall Street (line RR)

Buses
1, 6

Opening times
From end of March
Mon.–Fri. 9 a.m.–5 p.m.

*Cathedral Church of St John the Divine   C2

If it is ever completed, this church – the building of which began in 1891 – will be the largest in the world.

The first part of the church (apse, choir and crossing), designed by Heins and LaFarge, was in Byzantine-Romanesque style. After their death (1911) it was continued by Ralph Adams Cram on a new design for a Gothic cathedral. On the outbreak

Situation
Amsterdam Avenue and 112th Street

Subway station
116th Street (line 1)

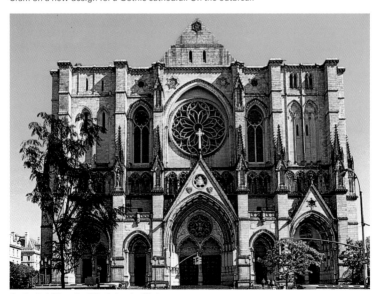

Cathedral Church of St John the Divine

Cathedral Church of Saint John the Divine
(Episcopal)

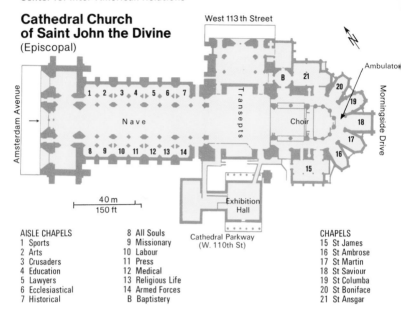

West 113th Street

Amsterdam Avenue

Nave

Transepts

Choir

Morningside Drive

Ambulatory

Exhibition Hall

Cathedral Parkway (W. 110th St)

40 m
150 ft

AISLE CHAPELS	8 All Souls	CHAPELS
1 Sports	9 Missionary	15 St James
2 Arts	10 Labour	16 St Ambrose
3 Crusaders	11 Press	17 St Martin
4 Education	12 Medical	18 St Saviour
5 Lawyers	13 Religious Life	19 St Columba
6 Ecclesiastical	14 Armed Forces	20 St Boniface
7 Historical	B Baptistery	21 St Ansgar

Bus
10

Opening times
Daily until dusk

Conducted tours
Mon.–Sat. 11 a.m. and
2 p.m.; Sun. 12.30 p.m.

of the Second World War, after another 30 years' work, building came to a halt. After the war work was resumed, but proceeded very slowly, and it was only at the end of the 1970s that a campaign got under way to collect money for the building of the towers.

The church is over 200 m (600 ft) long and some 100 m (300 ft) wide across the transepts. In a building of this size the mixture of styles is hardly noticeable, the Gothic element being predominant.

The interior is completely finished. A particularly notable feature is the baptistery.

There are conducted tours almost every day: for information tel. 678 6888.

Center for Inter-American Relations   E5

Address
680 Park Avenue

Subway station
68th Street (line 6)

Opening times
Tues.–Sun. noon–6 p.m.

The Center for Inter-American Relations is notable as the only art centre in New York devoted to the art of Central and South America. It puts on regular special exhibitions covering all periods from pre-Columbian to contemporary art. Here, too, lectures are given on the problems of Latin America.

Admission is free.

** Central Park

Central Park is the principal "lung" of New York City, with an area of 340 ha (840 acres), 5% of the total area of Manhattan. It extends for 4 km (2½ miles) from 59th to 110th Street, with a breadth of 500 m (550 yd) between Fifth Avenue and Central Park West, the continuation of Eighth Avenue.

The idea of a park for the rapidly growing city of New York was first put forward in the 1840s, and Central Park was laid out between 1859 and 1870 on a site which was then on the northern outskirts of the city. The layout was designed by Frederick Law Olmsted and Calvert Vaux, whose "Greensward Project" was selected following an open competition.

The construction of Central Park involved the removal of much stone and rock and the bringing in of 10 million waggon-loads of soil and humus. The park is now a natural monument, and no alteration of its layout is permitted.

The numerous bridges and the four sunken carriageways for through E–W traffic were part of the original plan. These roads were asphalted in 1912, and most of the footpaths were also asphalted soon afterwards. There are altogether some 30 miles of roads and footpaths in the park.

At weekends and at certain times on weekdays the whole of Central Park is closed to motor traffic, and the wide carriageways become the exclusive preserve of cyclists, roller skaters and the horse-drawn carriages which still operate in the park (cab-rank at S entrance, 59th Street).

The southern part of the park, which is much the most frequented, is an area of quieter and gentler beauty than the northern part (beyond 86th Street), which has been left in its natural state and is scenically more attractive. It is inadvisable to venture into this unfrequented northern area, even during the day, except in groups.

After dark the park should be avoided, except for theatrical and other events in summer.

In recent years the upkeep of Central Park has been rather neglected. This is partly due to the fact that it attracts large numbers of people during the summer months, particularly at weekends, and the staff are hard put to it to clear up after the thousands of visitors, in addition to which the care of damaged plants and trees and the repair of buildings make considerable demands on time and labour.

Just at the SE entrance (60th Street) is the Pond (bird sanctuary), and immediately N of this is the Wollman Memorial Rink (ice skating, roller-skating; occasionally used for rock concerts). Farther NE is a small zoo (at present under reconstruction), and to the NW of this runs the Mall, a straight avenue of elms lined with busts of writers and composers, including Shakespeare, Burns, Scott, Beethoven and Schiller.

To the W of the Mall extends Sheep Meadow, the finest expanse of grass in the park. From the end of the Mall a flight of steps leads down to the Bethesda Fountain and the Lake (hire of boats in summer). Immediately beyond this is a bicycle hire depot.

Subway stations
Fifth Avenue (lines N and RR), 59th Street (lines A, AA, CC and D), 72nd Street, 81st Street, 86th Street and 96th Street (lines AA and CC)

Buses
1, 2, 3, 4 and 103 (59th Street), 17 (79th Street), 18 (86th Street), 19 (96th Street), 29 (66th Street), 30 (72nd Street)

Pond, Wollman Rink, Zoo Mall

Sheep Meadow, Bethesda Fountain, Lake

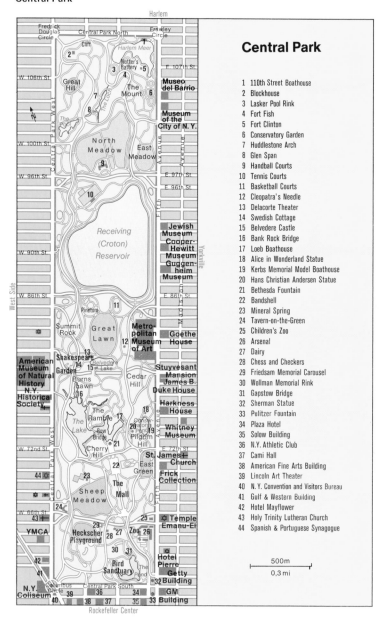

Central Park

1 110th Street Boathouse
2 Blockhouse
3 Lasker Pool Rink
4 Fort Fish
5 Fort Clinton
6 Conservatory Garden
7 Huddlestone Arch
8 Glen Span
9 Handball Courts
10 Tennis Courts
11 Basketball Courts
12 Cleopatra's Needle
13 Delacorte Theater
14 Swedish Cottage
15 Belvedere Castle
16 Bank Rock Bridge
17 Loeb Boathouse
18 Alice in Wonderland Statue
19 Kerbs Memorial Model Boathouse
20 Hans Christian Andersen Statue
21 Bethesda Fountain
22 Bandshell
23 Mineral Spring
24 Tavern-on-the-Green
25 Children's Zoo
26 Arsenal
27 Dairy
28 Chess and Checkers
29 Friedsam Memorial Carousel
30 Wollman Memorial Rink
31 Gapstow Bridge
32 Sherman Statue
33 Pulitzer Fountain
34 Plaza Hotel
35 Solow Building
36 N.Y. Athletic Club
37 Cami Hall
38 American Fine Arts Building
39 Lincoln Art Theater
40 N.Y. Convention and Visitors Bureau
41 Gulf & Western Building
42 Hotel Mayflower
43 Holy Trinity Lutheran Church
44 Spanish & Portuguese Synagogue

500m
0,3 mi

Central Park, New York's "Green Lung"

To the E of the Lake is the Conservatory Pond, the preserve of model yachts and motorboats. On its W side is a statue of Hans Christian Andersen, and to the N of this is a bronze group (by José de Creeft) of "Alice in Wonderland".

Conservatory Pond

Continuing NW, we come to Belvedere Castle (now a weather station), on the highest point in the park. Beyond this are the Belvedere Lake, surrounded by blossoming Japanese cherry-trees in mid April, and the Delacorte Theater, in which dramatic performances (admission free) are given in summer.

Belvedere Castle

The adjoining Great Lawn is used by young people for various ball games (baseball, football). In summer the Metropolitan perform operas here and the New York Philharmonic put on concerts.

Great Lawn

Behind the Metropolitan Museum of Art (see entry) is an Egyptian obelisk known as Cleopatra's Needle, sister to the obelisk of the same name in London, which was presented to New York by Khedive Ismail Pasha in the latter part of the 19th c. The obelisk is now badly weathered.

Cleopatra's Needle

Beyond the Great Lawn is the Reservoir, which occupies a quarter of the area of the park, extending from 86th Street to 97th Street. There is a pleasant walk around the Reservoir at any time of year.

Reservoir

To the N of the Reservoir there is much less in the way of man-made landscape: here nature has been left largely to itself. One attractively laid-out area, however, is the Conservatory Gardens (entrance at 105th Street and Fifth Avenue).

Conservatory Gardens

Harlem Meer

At the extreme NE end of the park is the Harlem Meer, a pond on which rowing-boats can be hired. Beyond 110th Street is the beginning of Harlem (see entry).

Catering facilities

There are a variety of facilities for eating and drinking in Central Park: the cafeteria in the Zoo (open 9 a.m.–5 p.m.); the Ice Cream Café and Deli on the E side of the Conservatory Pond (open 7.30 a.m.–8 p.m.); a small cafeteria on the Lake (open 9 a.m.–sunset); and the Tavern-on-the-Green, near the park entrance on Central Park West and 66th Street (open 11 a.m.–10 p.m., Sat. 11 a.m.–1 a.m. on Sun. morning, Sun. 10 a.m.–midnight; chamber music 11 a.m.–3 p.m.).
It is advisable to book a table at the Tavern-on-the-Green, particularly at weekends (tel. 873 3200).
During the warmer months of the year, and particularly at weekends, there are at least 50 frankfurter and hot-dog stalls in and around Central Park.

China House Gallery   E5

Address
125 East 65th Street

Subway station
68th Street (line 6)

Every year from mid March to the end of May and from October to January this gallery puts on outstanding exhibitions of classical Chinese art which are notable for their unity of theme (admission free).
The gallery is open on weekdays 10 a.m.–5 p.m., on Saturdays 11 a.m.–5 p.m. and on Sundays 2–5 p.m.

*Chinatown   E/F10

Subway stations
Canal Street (lines 6, N,
RR), City Hall (lines 4, 5, 6)

This exotic area, steadily expanding eastward and northward, is the largest Chinese town outside China, occupied by tens of thousands of Chinese, most of them living in apartment blocks a hundred or more years old and making a living by running their several hundred restaurants, foodshops and gift shops. Chinatown proper is bounded on the E by the Bowery (see entry), on the W by Baxter Street, on the N by Canal Street and on the S by Worth Street and Catham Square.
The first Chinese settlers were seamen who came to New York in the junk "Kee Ying" in 1847 and decided to stay. They were followed some 20–25 years later by unemployed Chinese coolies who had been working on the construction of the transcontinental railway to California and settled here on land belonging to John Mott and Joshua Pell.
Thereafter Chinese immigration was prevented by legislation, and it was only after the amendment of the immigration laws in 1965 that a further great influx of Chinese immigrants began. Thousands of the new arrivals found in this restricted area not only accommodation but employment – the men mainly in restaurants and shops, the women in some 300 small clothing factories.
In Chinatown there are some eight Chinese-language daily newspapers, all set by hand (compared with only five English papers), reflecting the political and regional differences and conflicts among the Chinese population.

Shop in Chinatown

On East Broadway (Nos. 11 and 75) are two C̣ ᵢese cinemas, mainly showing films from Hongkonᵣ ᵤd Taiwan in the original (sometimes with English s ᵤ.ties).
There is much of interest to be seen in a stroll through the narrow streets of Chinatown.

There are, for example, the Chinese Museum at 8 Mott Street (open daily 10 a.m.–6 p.m.) and a number of Buddhist temples, in particular one at 64 Mott Street.

Chinese Museum
(Chinatown Museum)

One notable event in the Chinese calendar is the celebration of the New Year (usually at the end of January to mid February), an occasion for noisy and colourful processions and the explosion of numerous firecrackers.
Information about life in Chinatown can be obtained from the Chinese Community Center, 62 Mott Street (tel. 267 5780), or the Chinese Community Cultural Center, 10 Confucius Plaza (tel. 925 2245).
Information about cultural events is supplied by the Chinese American Arts Council (tel. 431 9740).

*Chrysler Building   E6

The Chrysler Building, with which the automobile manufacturer Walter P. Chrysler sought to immortalise his name, was built in 1930, and for a year, until the completion of the Empire State Building in 1931, was New York's tallest skyscraper (319 m – 1045 ft high). It is still, however, the tallest building in New York to be scheduled as a national monument.

Address
425 Lexington Avenue

Subway station
Grand Central (lines 4, 5, 6, 7)

The Chrysler Building has been seen as a symbol of the romantic yearnings of New Yorkers, who feel more at home with this elegantly conceived skyscraper than with the uncompromisingly rectangular World Trade Center (see entry) which now dominates the city's skyline.

The Chrysler Building's most striking feature, visible from all over the city, is the sharply pointed spire with its arches and triangular windows of stainless steel. The Art Deco style which inspired the architect, William Van Alen, to create this unusual building, which when first constructed was decried as eccentric and bizarre, is seen also in the entrance hall and the 18 lifts (with different patterns of intarsia decoration), which have been restored to their original condition.

On the 66th floor (out of the Chrysler Building's total of 77) is the Cloud Club restaurant, due to be reopened after a long period of closure. There is no viewing terrace.

Buses
104, 106

Opening times
During office hours

*City Hall   E11

City Hall, in a style which shows a mixture, unusual in America, of French Renaissance and neo-classicism, was completed in 1812 after a building period of nine years. It was designed by the French architect Joseph-François Mangin and the New Yorker John McComb, winners of a competition which brought them the large premium of 350 dollars.

Marble from Massachusetts was used on the main front and the ends of the building; the rear was more economically finished in the ubiquitous New York brownstone. The exterior was so ravaged by air pollution and pigeon dropping, however, that the building had to be refaced with Alabama sandstone in 1959.

City Hall houses municipal council chambers and offices. The only parts open to the public are the entrance hall, the Rotunda, the grand staircase and the Governor's Room.

The Governor's Room was used by the governor of New York State when he visited New York from the State capital at Albany. It is now a museum, containing furniture made for the original City Hall and pictures of historical interest.

The public are admitted to the sessions of the City Council and the Board of Estimate (the city's second chamber), which meet in City Hall.

Situation
City Hall Park, Broadway

Subway stations
Brooklyn Bridge (lines 4, 5, 6), Park Place (lines 2, 3), City Hall (line RR)

Buses
1, 6

Opening times
Mon.–Fri. 10 a.m.–3.30 p.m.

Civic Center   E10/11

This complex of municipal, State and Federal offices, situated near City Hall, shows a characteristic New York mixture of every conceivable architectural style. The most notable buildings are the following.

Brooklyn Bridge (lines 4, 5, 6)

◀ *An Art Deco skyscraper – the Chrysler Building*

Civic Center

City Hall

Municipal Building	The Municipal Building, standing at the corner of Chambers Street and Centre Street immediately above the subway station, was built in 1914 by the well-known New York firm of architects McKim, Mead and White. This 36-storey skyscraper seeks to adapt older architectural styles to modern use and is topped by a copper statue, recently regilded, of "Civic Virtue" (by Adolph Weinman).
Tweed Courthouse	This building, at 52 Chambers Street, is named after one of New York's most notorious political bosses. Designed by John Kellum in the style of an Anglo-Italian palazzo, it was completed in 1872. The building (entrance in basement) is now rather the worse for wear.
Surrogate's Court	The Surrogate's Court Building (31 Chambers Street) was erected in 1911 and is one of the numerous public buildings in New York in the "Beaux Arts" style. The façade is of striking effect.
Police Headquarters	Standing opposite the Municipal Building and linked with it by a plaza, the Police Headquarters, built by Gruzen and Partners in 1973, is the most recent structure in the Civic Center.
United States Courthouse	The United States Courthouse, seat of the Federal District Court, occupies a central position in the Civic Center. Built in 1936, it was designed by Cass Gilbert, architect of the Woolworth Building (see entry), and his son.
New York County Courthouse	Opposite the United States Courthouse is the New York County Courthouse (by Guy Lowell, 1912), a hexagonal building with a façade in the style of a Roman temple.

On the opposite side of the square stands the Federal Office Building, erected in 1967 by Alfred Easton Poor, Kahn and Eggers. With its numerous small windows the façade has something of the appearance of a chessboard.

Federal Office Building

The Criminal Courts Building, at 100 Centre Street, designed by Harley Wiley Corbett in a style reminiscent of the German "Neue Sachlichkeit" of the inter-war years, was erected in 1939. The old Tombs Prison has been closed for many years.

Criminal Courts Building and Tombs Prison

* * The Cloisters

The Cloisters, built in 1938 to the design of the Boston architect Charles Collens, combine fragments of European buildings of the 12th–15th c. with modern architecture but contrive in masterly fashion to blend these diverse elements into a unified whole. The tower is modelled on that of the 12th c. French monastery of St Michel-de-Cuxa in the Pyrenees, a cloister from which is incorporated in the building.
The Cloisters are a branch of the Metropolitan Museum of Art (see entry), housing its collection of medieval art. Most of the works of art displayed here were presented to the Metropolitan by John D. Rockefeller Jr (1874–1960), who also financed the construction of the Cloisters in Fort Tryon Park, which he had previously presented to the city. From the Cloisters there is a magnificent view, in clear weather, of the Hudson river. Information: tel. 923 3700.

Situation
Fort Tryon Park

Subway station
190th Street (line A)

Bus
4

Opening times
Tues.–Sat. 10 a.m.–
4.45 p.m.; Sun. and holidays,
noon (or 1 p.m.)–4.45 p.m.

In order to get a general view of medieval art in chronological order, the best plan is to start in the Romanesque Hall (doorways from French churches and monasteries; sculpture) and continue as follows:

Main Floor

Fuentidueña Chapel
The apse of this chapel, which contains Romanesque art from Spain and France, comes from the Spanish church of San Martín de Fuentidueña.

St Guilhem Cloister
Columns and capitals from the Benedictine abbey of St Guilhem-le-Désert near Montpellier.

Langon Chapel
Parts of the Romanesque church of Notre-Dame du Bourg at Langon, near Bordeaux.

Pontaut Chapter House
A complete chapter house from a Benedictine (later Cistercian) abbey in Gascony.

Cuxa Cloister
A cloister (partly original, partly reconstructed) from a Benedictine abbey in the Pyrenees which was dissolved during the French Revolution.

Nine Heroes Tapestry Room
14th c. French tapestries (probably by Nicolas Bataille) depicting the Nine Heroes of medieval legend. Five of the heroes survive (Alexander the Great, Caesar, David, Joshua

MAIN FLOOR

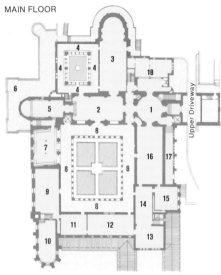

GROUND FLOOR

The Cloisters

Museum of Medieval Religious Art and Architecture

MAIN FLOOR

1 Entrance Hall
2 Romanesque Hall
   (Doorways from France)
3 Fuentidueña Chapel
   (Apse from the church of San Martin de Fuentidueña, near Segovia)
4 St-Guilhem Cloister
   (Cloister from the Benedictine abbey of St Guilhem-le-Désert in southern France)
5 Langon Chapel
   (Parts of the church of Notre-Dame du Bourg, Langon, SW France)
6 West Terrace
7 Pontaut Chapter House
   (Chapter house of the abbey of Notre-Dame de Pontaut, SW France)
8 Cuxa Cloister
   (Cloister, partly reconstructed, from the monastery of St Michel-de-Cuxa in the French Pyrenees)
9 Early Gothic Hall
   (Figures of saints)
10 Gothic Chapel
   See Ground Floor
11 Nine Heroes Tapestry Room
12 Hall of Unicorn Tapestries
13 Boppard Room
   Stained glass from the Carmelite convent of St Severin, Boppard am Rhein)
14 Burgos Room
   (Flemish tapestry from Burgos Cathedral)
15 Spanish Room (Campin Room)
   (Merode altarpiece, an "Annunciation" by Robert Campin; Gothic ceiling paintings from Castile)
16 Late-Gothic Hall
   (In the style of a medieval refectory)
17 Froville Arcade
   (Gothic arcade from Froville priory, Lorraine)
18 Books and reproductions

GROUND FLOOR
1 Gothic Chapel
   (Modelled on the Gothic Cathedral of St-Nazaire, Carcassonne)
2 Bonnefont Cloister
   (Two arcades from the abbey of Bonnefont-en-Comminges, SW France)
3 Trie Cloister
   (From the convent of Trie, near Toulouse)
4 Glass Gallery
5 Treasury

In the Cloisters

and King Arthur); the missing ones are Hector, Judas Maccabaeus, Charlemagne and Godfrey of Bouillon.

Early Gothic Hall
French and Italian sculpture; 14th c. Italian paintings.

Boppard Room
Six panels of 15th c. stained glass from the Carmelite church at Boppard, on the Rhine.

Hall of the Unicorn Tapestries
Five out of a set of seven tapestries woven in the last year of the 15th c. for the marriage of Louis XII of France with Anne de Bretagne. They depict the hunt and capture of the unicorn, a medieval symbol of purity.

Burgos Tapestry Room
In this room is the only surviving tapestry out of a set of eight, woven for the Emperor Maximilian in 1495, which formerly belonged to Burgos Cathedral.

Spanish Room (Campin Room)
The painted wooden ceiling comes from a palace near Madrid.

Late Gothic Hall
This hall, in the style of a medieval refectory, contains stained glass, reredoses and sculpture of the 15th and 16th c.

Froville Arcade
A Gothic arcade from the Benedictine priory of Froville in eastern France.

Cooper-Hewitt Museum

Ground Floor

Gothic Chapel
Modelled on the Cathedral of St-Nazaire in Carcassonne.

Bonnefont Cloister
This incorporates two arcades from a Cistercian abbey in the French Pyrenees.

Trie Cloister
Marble capitals from the 15th c. convent of Trie near Tarbes in SW France, destroyed by Huguenots in the 16th c. Reproduction of the original cloister garden.

Glass Gallery
Stained glass, sculpture; courtyard from a house in Abbeville.

Treasury
Small objects of religious art of the 12th–15th c.; two pictures by a pupil of Rogier van der Weyden.

Cooper-Hewitt Museum
E3

Situation
Fifth Avenue and 91st Street

Subway station
86th Street (lines 4, 5, 6)

Buses
1, 2, 3, 4

Opening times
Tues. 10 a.m.–9 p.m.,
Wed.–Sat. 10 a.m.–5 p.m.
Sun. and public holidays
noon–5 p.m.

Admission charge
Free Tues. after 5 p.m.

The only museum of design in New York, the Cooper-Hewitt Museum belongs to the group of museums run by the Smithsonian Institution, whose other major museums are in Washington.
Although the Cooper-Hewitt collection was established in 1897, it was housed until 1963 in the Cooper Union in southern Manhattan and was not open to the public. It is now located in the former Carnegie Mansion, one of the few detached private houses in Manhattan, which was built by the Scottish-born steel king Andrew Carnegie in 1901 and was occupied by the Carnegie family until 1949. Thereafter the house was used by Columbia University, and finally was presented by the Carnegie Foundation to the Smithsonian.
A sumptuous mansion in a version of Renaissance style, originally containing 64 rooms, the house was renovated and reconstructed for the purposes of the Museum in 1977. The collection includes wallpaper, textiles, furniture, glass, china, jewellery, clothing, drawings and prints, and there is also a large picture reference archive. The Museum puts on periodic special exhibitions.

Dyckman House

Situation
Broadway and 204th Street

Subway stations
207th Street (line A),
Dyckman Street (line 1)

Buses
104 (to 125th Street), then 5
(to 168th Street and 200th
Street)

Opening times
Tues.–Sun. 11 a.m.–5 p.m.

Admission free

The only farmhouse which still survives in Manhattan is the Dyckman House, built in 1783 on the site of an earlier house destroyed during the War of American Independence.
Built by William Dyckman, grandson of a Westphalian named Jan Dyckman who had emigrated to New Amsterdam, the house remained until 1915 in the hands of the Dyckman family, who then presented it to the city.
In the basement of the house is the winter kitchen, on the ground floor living rooms, on the upper floor five bedrooms, and above this an attic.
The house contains the original 18th c. furniture. The garden behind the house, restored to its original form, still has one of the cherry-trees for which the Dyckman farm was famed.

Dyckman House, Manhattan's last surviving farmhouse

Ellis Island

Ellis Island

Subway stations
South Ferry (line 1),
Whitehall Street (line RR),
Bowling Green (line 6)

Boat
From Battery Park,
end Apr. to end Oct., daily at
9.30 a.m., 11.45 a.m., 2 p.m.
and 4.15 p.m.

Ellis Island, one of the 40 islands in the waters round New York, was famous between 1890 and 1917 as the point of entry for immigrants to the United States. There are now conducted tours of the island, starting on the arrival of the Circle Line boats. The whole trip to and from the island and including the conducted tour takes $1\frac{1}{2}$ to 2 hours, and affords magnificent views of Manhattan – better than the views to be had from other boat trips (Circle Line sightseeing cruise, sail to Liberty Island, Staten Island ferry).

This "island of tears", as it was known to immigrants detained here, was vacated in 1954 but has only been open to sightseers since 1976. The conducted tour still gives an excellent idea of the methods of dealing with immigrants in the early years of this century. (In 1907 no fewer than 1,285,239 people passed through Ellis Island.)

During the two world wars Ellis Island was used as a place of internment for aliens.

* * Empire State Building   D7

Fifth Avenue and 34th Street

34th Street (lines B, D, F, N
and RR), 33rd Street (lines
2, 3, 4, 5, 6 and 16)

1, 2, 3, 4, 5

Daily 9.30 a.m.–midnight

Although now exceeded in height by the World Trade Center (see entry), the Empire State Building, erected in 1931, is still the principal emblem and landmark of New York. From its two observatories (viewing terraces) on the 86th and 102nd floors there are incomparable views over Manhattan, extending in clear weather to other parts of the city and the neighbouring state of New Jersey.

Built of sandstone and granite, the Empire State Building is in some ways a vertical city in itself, with a total height of 448 m (1472 ft) to the tip of the television aerial on its summit. The stainless-steel window framing gives it a characteristic glitter both by day and by night. The upper 30 floors are illuminated from 9 p.m. to midnight by powerful coloured floodlights.

The ascent of the Empire State Building is equally rewarding either during the day or in the evening. In hazy weather, such as New York frequently experiences during the summer, it is best to go early in the day.

Guinness World Records Exhibit Hall

Daily 9.30 a.m.–6 p.m.

This interesting exhibition, on the ground floor of the Empire State Building, contains a variety of exhibits and displays (including video films) illustrating the unusual achievements and statistics recorded in the "Guinness Book of Records".

Federal Hall National Memorial   E11

Address
25 Wall Street

This building at the junction of Wall Street and Nassau Street, originally the City Custom House, was completed in 1842 after

Empire State Building ▶

Fifth Avenue

Subway stations
Wall Street (lines 4, 5),
Rector Street (line RR)

Buses
1, 6

Opening times
Mon.–Fri. 9 a.m.–4.30 p.m.

a building period of eight years. It marks the high point of Greek Revival architecture in New York.

The Wall Street façade of the building, conceived in the style of a Doric temple, is like a simplified version of the Parthenon, without a frieze. The interior is in the form of a rotunda, more Roman than Greek in inspiration.

From 1862 to 1920 Federal Hall was occupied by a department of the US Treasury. In 1955 it became a National Memorial, commemorating the fact that George Washington was inaugurated as first President of the United States on this spot in 1789. The site was then occupied by New York's old City Hall, built in 1701 and modernised by Pierre L'Enfant, famous as the planner of the new federal capital in Washington.

**Fifth Avenue

E1–9

Subway stations
Fifth Avenue/60th Street
(lines N, RR), Fifth Avenue/
53rd Street (lines E, F), Fifth
Avenue/42nd Street (line 7)

Buses
1, 2, 3, 4, 103 (59th Street),
28 (57th Street), 29 (50th
Street), 106 (42nd Street),
16 (34th Street)

Fifth Avenue, in particular the section between 59th and 34th Street (roughly 2 km (1¼ miles) in length), is New York's best known thoroughfare, a magnificent avenue which has an endless fascination for visitors, as well as for New Yorkers. Among its attractions are numerous luxury shops, banks, airline offices, churches, the Rockefeller Center, the New York Public Library, the Empire State Building (see entries) and much else besides. Fifth Avenue divides Manhattan into an eastern and a western part, and since New York lacks any large central squares it is the real centre of the city. A stroll along Fifth Avenue is an essential element in the process of getting to know New York.

On Fifth Avenue

While walking along Fifth Avenue do not forget to look along some of the side streets, such as 47th Street West, home of the diamond trade, in which Hassidic Jews have a virtual monopoly, or 46th Street West, which has become a kind of Little Brazil. From the corner of 43rd Street there is a particularly fine view of the Chrysler Building (see entry).

Side streets

Apart from the buildings which have an entry to themselves in this guide, Fifth Avenue has few other individual buildings of particular interest. In general it would be true to say that it is more interesting for its total effect than for its separate parts. Worth a look in passing, however, are the Plaza Hotel (59th Street: see Practical Information, Hotels), in the style of a French château (by Henry J. Hardenbergh, 1907); the Corning Glass Building (No. 717, corner of 56th Street), designed by Harrison and Abramowitz, architects of the Rockefeller Center (see entry) and the Metropolitan Opera in the Lincoln Center – see entry (see Practical Information, Music); the Metropolitan Club at the corner of 60th Street, in the style of a Florentine palazzo (by Stanford White, 1893); and the University Club at the corner of 54th Street (by Charles F. McKim, 1899).
At the corner of 52nd Street is the last survivor of the mansions built in this area at the beginning of the 20th c. by wealthy families such as the Astors, Vanderbilts and Goulds; the building is now occupied by Cartier, the internationally known jewellers.

Notable buildings

Fraunces' Tavern

E12

Fraunces' Tavern opened in 1719 and was the first restaurant in the US. George Washington spent his last days here as general of the American forces in the winter of 1783 before taking farewell of his officers and retiring to his estate at Mount Vernon, near the future capital of the Union which was to bear his name. Thomas Jefferson had his offices there when he was Secretary of State during the late 18th c. The present inn, a faithful restoration of the original built in 1928, is now a popular restaurant. On the upper floors are a museum containing mementoes of the American revolution and a library of 4000 volumes and manuscripts relating to the revolution and to the history of New York.

Address
54 Pearl Street

Subway stations
Bowling Green (lines 4, 5), South Ferry (line 1), Wall Street (lines 3, 4)

Bus
15 (to Broad Street)

Opening times
Mon.–Fri. 10 a.m.–4 p.m.

Admission free

**Frick Collection

E5

The Frick Collection, assembled by the German-American steel magnate Henry Clay Frick, is housed in the mansion built in 1914 as his residence. It was opened to the public in 1935, 16 years after Frick's death. The house is typical of the numerous palatial mansions built by millionaires on Fifth Avenue, a number of which still survive, though now converted to other uses.
The house has 40 rooms altogether, and the collection is displayed in the 16 ground-floor rooms, which have preserved much of the character of a private residence. Frick's original collection of 130 pictures, sculpture and fine furniture has been

Address
1 East 70th Street

Subway station
72nd Street (line 6)

Buses
1, 2, 3, 4

Opening times
Tues.–Sat. 10 a.m.–6 p.m., Sun. 1–6 p.m., often closed on Tues. in July and August

supplemented over the past 45 years by the addition of relatively few new works, but all of the highest quality. The Frick Collection is very different, therefore, from the normal art gallery. Here there is no attempt at systematic grouping or chronological order: the main consideration in the arrangement of the pictures and other works of art has been asethetic effect.

Boucher Room
This room, in the style of a French boudoir, contains eight pictures by Boucher, painted for Madame de Pompadour's boudoir in the château of Crécy.

Dining Room
Furnished as it was in Frick's lifetime, with 18th c. English paintings.

South Hall
Two pictures by Vermeer; Renoir's "Mother and Children"; console table by Gouthière; secretaire by Riesener.

West Vestibule
Boucher's "Four Seasons", painted for Madame de Pompadour.

Fragonard Room
Eleven pictures by Fragonard.

Living Hall
Pictures by El Greco ("St Jerome"), Titian ("Man in a Red Cap" and "Pietro Aretino") and Holbein ("Sir Thomas More" and "Thomas Cromwell").

Library
Pictures by Gainsborough and Lawrence; Italian Renaissance bronzes.

North Hall
Van Eyck's "Virgin and Child, with Saints and Donor".

Frick Collection

The Frick Collection is displayed on the ground floor of the mansion built for Henry Clay Frick (1849–1919) in 1913–14, on a site previously occupied by the Lenox Library. The house was designed by Thomas Hastings in a style reminiscent of 18th c. European domestic architecture.

1 Entrance Hall	10 South Hall
2 Reception Hall	11 Library
3 Sales Room	12 North Hall
4 Boucher Room	13 Portico
5 Anteroom	14 Enamel Room
6 Dining Room	15 Oval Room
7 West Vestibule	16 Garden Court
8 East Vestibule	17 Green Room
9 Fragonard Room	18 Terrace

West Gallery
Pictures by El Greco, Goya, Rembrandt and Velázquez and one of the few works in America by de la Tour.

Oval Room
Portraits by Van Dyck and Gainsborough.

East Gallery
Pictures by Claude Lorrain ("Sermon on the Mount") and Ingres ("Comtesse d'Haussonville"); portraits by Goya, Drouais, David and Whistler.

Garden Court
This courtyard, with a vaulted glass roof and a beautiful fountain, contains busts by Houdon and Barbet.

Lecture Hall
This contains a collection of books on art.

*Gracie Mansion   F3

The Gracie Mansion, since 1942 the residence of the Mayor of New York City, was originally built in 1799 for a Scottish importer named Archibald Gracie but was much altered and enlarged in subsequent years, most recently in 1966. It has been open to the public since the autumn of 1980.

The house had many owners before being acquired by the city in 1891. From 1925 to 1935 it was occupied by the Museum of the City of New York (see entry).

The Carl Schurz Park, named after New York's best-known 19th c. German immigrant, is one of the city's most pleasant little green oases.

Situation
Carl Schurz Park, at end of East 88th Street

Bus
19

Opening times
Apr.–Oct., Wed. 10 a.m.– 4 p.m.

*Greenwich Village   D/E9

Greenwich Village, known to its inhabitants simply as "the Village", has preserved nothing of the village-like character it must have had when it first grew up in the 18th c. This area on the W side of Broadway, between 14th Street in the N and Houston Street in the S, became known in the first 30 years or so of this century as the centre of New York's *vie de Bohème* and was inhabited by intellectuals, writers and artists, who found cheap lodgings here and frequented its little theatres and numerous cafés. In those days there were no buildings higher than three or four storeys, rents were low, and the residents felt that they had little to do with the rest of New York.

The number of writers and artists who have lived in the Village is legion. Among the writers have been James Fenimore Cooper, Theodore Dreiser, Willa Cather, Edgar Allan Poe, Richard Wright, Henry James, Edith Wharton, John Dos Passos, Marianne Moore, Mark Twain, Sinclair Lewis, Dorothy Thompson, Thomas Wolfe, Hart Crane, Mary McCarthy, E. E. Cummings, William Styron and Edward Albee; among the artists Edward Hopper, William Glackens and Rockwell Kent. Only a few houses, however, have plaques commemorating former famous residents.

Subway stations
4th Street (lines A, AA, B, D, E, F), Sheridan Square (line 1), 8th Street (line RR)

Buses
2, 3, 6

Greenwich Village: Washington Square

Greenwich Village has now become a respectable residential area: although many of the old low houses still survive there are now numerous modern apartment blocks and the rents are among the highest in New York (second only to Upper East Side), while the little restaurants (mainly French and Italian) are just as dear as those in other parts of the city. In other words the Village has now been fully integrated into New York.

Washington Square

Once a place of execution, a paupers' cemetery and a drill ground, Washington Square is now the principal square of the Village, the scene of constant bustle and activity, particularly at weekends when it becomes a kind of microcosm of the whole city, with people of all races, nations and ages playing, making music, roller skating or merely sitting quietly in the sun.

Main Street

Main Street, 8th Street, leads E from the Avenue of the Americas to Broadway; between Fifth Avenue and the Avenue of the Americas it is particularly interesting because of its lively atmosphere.

Bleecker Street

This is another interesting street, with numerous antique shops, restaurants, night spots, cinemas and theatres.

Other streets

After Bleecker Street the most interesting streets are Mac-Dougal Street, with MacDougal Alley, which branches off near 8th Street; Minetta Lane; Bedford Street, at No. 75 of which is the oldest house in the Village (1799); Commerce Street, Grove Street and Sheridan Square; Christopher Street, the haunt of homosexuals; St Luke's Place (between Leroy and Hudson Streets), with a group of houses dating from 1855, still in their original form; and Hudson Street, with the church of St Luke in

East Village

the Fields (No. 485). The church, built in 1822, still has something of the air of a village church in spite of later alterations; it was badly damaged by fire in 1981. In this part of Hudson Street there are many antique shops, selling mainly Americana.

This striking building at the corner of the Avenue of the Americas and 10th Street, in a splendidly exuberant Venetian Gothic, was erected in 1876 and until 1945 served as a courthouse. In 1967 it was reopened as a branch of the New York Public Library (see entry).

Jefferson Market Library

This square, on the northern edge of the Village, was the entertainment quarter of New York around the turn of the 19th–20th c., with numerous theatres and hotels and some of the city's best shops. It is now much in need of rehabilitation. On the N side of Union Square, at 860 Broadway, is Andy Warhol's famous "Factory"; and the artist himself can occasionally be seen at the market which is held in the square every Saturday from May to December.

Union Square

As Greenwich Village became increasingly fashionable its less prosperous residents moved E. During the 1960s St Mark's Place, the continuation of 8th Street, became the great centre of activity of the "flower people", and this area was christened East Village; but little is now to be seen of this short-lived phenomenon. At the end of the 19th c. East Village was much favoured by German immigrants. There are now many Ukrainians in this area, with Ukrainian shops, restaurants and meeting-places, as well as a church (which was established in

East Village

1977) in 7th Street, between Second and Third Avenues.
The poet W. H. Auden lived at 60 St Mark's Place in his last
years.

Grey Art Gallery and Study Center   E9

Address
33 Washington Place

Subway stations
West 4th Street (lines A, B,
D, E, F, AA, CC),
8th Street (line RR),
Astor Place (line 6)

Buses
1, 2, 3, 5, 6

This gallery, opened in the autumn of 1977 belongs to New
York University and houses the University's permanent art
collection, made up solely of works presented or bequeathed to
it. It consists mainly of American art from 1940 to the present
day, but there is also a collection of contemporary art from
Turkey, Iran, India and Japan. The gallery also puts on
interesting special exhibitions.

The Grey Gallery is open from September to the end of May on
Tuesdays and Thursdays 10 a.m.–6.30 p.m. and Wednesdays
10 a.m.–8.30 p.m.; in June, July and August it is open
Monday–Friday 11 a.m.–7 p.m. Admission free.

* *Guggenheim Museum   E3

Situation
Fifth Avenue and 89th Street

Subway station
86th Street (lines 4, 5, 6)

Buses
1, 2, 3, 4

Opening times
Tues. 11 a.m.–8 p.m.,
Wed.–Sun. and holidays
11 a.m.–5 p.m.

Admission free
Tues. after 5 p.m.

The Solomon R. Guggenheim Museum began life in 1937 as
the Museum for Non-Objective Art, but was soon renamed
after its founder, an enormously wealthy copper magnate, and
given wider terms of reference as a museum of modern art.
In 1943 Guggenheim commissioned the famous architect
Frank Lloyd Wright (who had not as yet erected any buildings
in New York) to build a museum on this site; but it was another
16 years before it was completed, since the municipal
authorities kept imposing fresh conditions before finally
approving the plan. By the time the museum was opened
Guggenheim was dead and Frank Lloyd Wright was 88.

This is the only New York museum which is as famous for its
architecture as for its contents. Wright saw a museum as an
organic structure consisting of a single large room on one
continuous floor. In this case the continuous floor is a spiral
ramp 432 m (473 yd) long. Visitors are taken up to the top of
the museum in a lift and then walk down the ramp to the exit.
The only natural light in the museum comes from the glass roof
30 m (100 ft) above the ground; there are no windows, and few
seats on which visitors can rest on the way down.

The Guggenheim Museum puts on five or six special
exhibitions a year, many of which occupy the whole museum.
On these occasions the visitor will look in vain for the
permanent collection, although this stock of over 4000 works
(listed in the Museum's comprehensive catalogue) would be
highly valued by any other museum concerned with the art of
the last hundred years. The collection includes, for example, 72
works by Kandinsky, several dozen paintings and watercolours
by Klee and pictures by Picasso, Léger, Braque, Delaunay and
Chagall. Notable among the sculpture are fine works by
Archipenko, Brancuși and Calder.

An extension completed in 1980 has provided a number of
small rooms in which at least part of the permanent collection
can be displayed, the works on show being changed every few
months.

Also on permanent display, outside the main spiral, is a
collection of 75 pictures assembled by the Munich art dealer

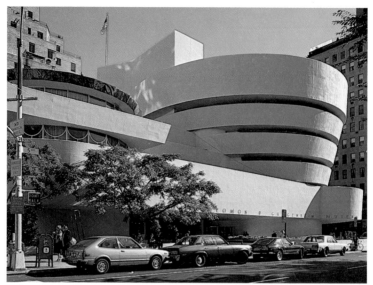

Guggenheim Museum

Guggenheim Museum: interior

Justin K. Thannhäuser. This consists mainly of French paintings from the Impressionists (Manet, Pissarro, Renoir, Cézanne, Gauguin, etc.) to Picasso, who is represented by many of his early works.

Guinness World Records Exhibit Hall

See Empire State Building

Harlem   D/E1

Subway stations
125th Street (lines 4, 5),
125th Street and Lenox
Avenue (lines 2, 3)

Buses
2, 5, 10

In spite of its reputation as a ghetto, and of the rather down-at-heel appearance of many parts of this area in east central Manhattan, Harlem is better off than some other quarters of New York. Bounded on the S by 110th Street (called Central Park North in the section running along the N end of Central Park), on the E by Madison Avenue, on the N by 150th Street and on the W by Eighth Avenue, Harlem consists mainly – apart from a number of contemporary skyscrapers – of houses built about the turn of the 19th and 20th c. for the prosperous middle classes. The houses are better built than in other parts of Manhattan, and the streets (such as Lenox Avenue, which with 125th Street forms the real centre of Harlem) are wider than any others in New York. As a result of overbuilding, however, the houses could not be let, and a black estate agent persuaded the owners to accept as tenants the blacks who were being driven out of their slum dwellings in southern Manhattan by the steady commercial development of that area. By about 1910 the population of Harlem was almost entirely black.

Nowadays little is left to bear witness to the splendours of Harlem's early days. Numbers of empty houses, some of them burned out and boarded up, give many Harlem streets the appearance of an area which has recently suffered an air raid. The effect of the high unemployment rate – traditionally higher among blacks than among whites, and here particularly affecting the young – also makes itself felt here: nowhere else are to be seen so many men with nothing to do as in Harlem, particularly during the warmer months of the year.

The question is often asked: is it safe to go about Harlem on foot? The answer must be that it is safe, provided that you bear one or two rules in mind. Do not go in large parties, and do not take photographs of the people of Harlem or stare at them, since this might reasonably cause offence. You should visit Harlem in the evening only if you have a particular destination in mind, such as a jazz club, a dance hall or a theatre. If you wish to visit Harlem on your own best plan is to go on one of the three-hour bus tours of Harlem run by the (black) Penny Sightseeing Co. or one of the Harlem Renaissance Tours (see Practical Information, Sightseeing tours). On these tours experienced guides will point out the positive as well as the negative aspects of Harlem, and you will be told where you can take photographs and where you should not. After a trip of this kind you may even be tempted to come back and have another look on your own: once you know the area you may be less hampered by the inhibitions and apprehensions which can be

Harlem: the cheerful face of a black ghetto

aroused by sensational reports in the press and on television. The best place to go for literature by and about blacks is the Liberation Bookstore (Lenox Avenue and 131st Street).

"There is so much to see in Harlem," said Langston Hughes, a leading black writer who lived there for many years; and certainly the visitor to Harlem will have the feeling of being in quite a different world from the one he is accustomed to.

Among recently erected buildings in Harlem are the two high-rise apartment blocks, built in 1975, on the Arthur A. Schomburg Plaza (110th and 111th Streets, between Fifth and Madison Avenues); the New York State Office Building (163 West 125th Street); Lenox Terrace (between Fifth and Lenox Avenues and 132nd and 135th Streets), the largest housing estate in Harlem (1957); the Schomburg Center for Research in Black Culture (see entry), corner of Lenox Avenue and 135th Street, completed in 1980; Riverbend, one of the finest modern housing estates in New York (on Fifth Avenue, between 138th and 142nd Streets: 1967); and the Harlem School of the Arts (645 St Nicholas Street, on 141st Street: 1977).

New buildings

The most interesting of Harlem's older buildings are the numerous churches, including the Church of St Thomas the Apostle (1907), at 260 West 118th Street; St Martin's Episcopal Church (1888), at the corner of 122nd Street and Lenox Avenue; the Bethel Gospel Pentecostal Assembly (1889), at 36 West 123rd Street, a fine neo-Romanesque church which was formerly occupied by the Harlem Club; and the Ephesus Seventh Day Adventist Church (1887), at 267 Lenox Avenue, originally a Dutch Reformed church.

Churches

One church particularly worth seeing is All Saints (1894), at the corner of Madison Avenue and 129th Street, which was designed by James Renwick, architect of the Grace Church and St Patrick's Cathedral. Perhaps the best known of all Harlem's churches, however, is the Abyssinian Baptist Church, at 132 West 138th Street, in which Adam Clayton Powell and his son of the same name (who was also a member of Congress) preached their fiery sermons.

The Williams Christian Methodist Episcopal Church (2225 Seventh Avenue, between 131st and 132nd Streets) is of interest only because it has taken over the Lafayette Theater, which was the best known black theatre between 1910 and 1940.

A black Jewish congregation, the Ethiopian Hebrew Congregation, meets in a 90-year-old neo-Renaissance mansion at 1 West 123rd Street.

Dance Theater of Harlem	The Dance Theater of Harlem, directed by Arthur Mitchell, occupies a former garage at 466 West 152nd Street, converted for the purpose in 1971.
Malcolm Shabazz Mosque No. 7	The old Lenox Casino at 102 West 116th Street became in 1965 Muhammad's Temple of Islam. Following a split in this black sect it is now the Malcolm Shabazz Mosque No. 7.
Strivers' Row	Harlem possesses two apartment blocks which are among the finest in the whole of New York. They lie on 138th and 139th Streets, between Adam C, Powell Jr Boulevard and Seventh Avenue, and are known as Strivers' Row. These well-preserved and partly restored blocks were built in 1891 by four firms of architects for a contractor who set out to show that good and roomy houses could be built at a reasonable price.
Apollo Theater	The famous Apollo Theater at 223 West 125th Street, one of New York's great temples of jazz in which many black musicians performed, was converted into a cinema in the early 1970s. This marked the end of an era in Harlem show business, which had begun to flourish so remarkably in the twenties and thirties. The Apollo was opened in 1913, but no blacks were admitted until 1934. Among the galaxy of stars who performed here in the next 40 years were Bessie Smith, Billie Holiday, Huddie Ledbetter, Duke Ellington, Count Basie, Dizzie Gillespie, Thelonius Monk and Aretha Franklin.

Hayden Planetarium

See American Museum of Natural History

Hispanic Society of America Museum

Situation
Broadway and 155th Street

Subway stations
157th Street (line 1),
155th Street (lines AA, CC)

The museum and its library are devoted to the cultures of the Spanish-speaking peoples from prehistoric times to the present day. The pictures include works by El Greco, Velázquez and Goya, and there is a rich collection of applied art and crafts, including pottery, tiles, ironwork and silver.

Opening times: Tuesday–Saturday 10 a.m.–4.30 p.m., Sunday 1–4 p.m.; closed Monday. The Museum is also usually closed on public holidays.

Admission free

Jacques Marchais Center of Tibetan Art

This collection of Tibetan art, the largest in the West, is difficult to get to but is well worth the trouble for anyone with interests in this field. Assembled by a woman art dealer of New York, it is housed in a building modelled on a Tibetan monastery.
In addition to Tibetan art, which constitutes the main part of the collection, there are also examples of Chinese, Japanese, Indian and Persian art.
Opening times are: Sat. and Sun. 1–5 p.m.

Address
338 Lighthouse Avenue,
Staten Island

Boat
Staten Island ferry from
Battery Park and bus R 113

Japan House Gallery   F6

This gallery puts on special exhibitions periodically of Japanese art of high quality.
The building, designed in Japanese style, also contains a theatre in which there are frequent showings of Japanese films and occasional lectures.
The gallery is open daily, 11 a.m.–5 p.m.; Friday 11 a.m.–7.30 p.m.

Address
333 East 47th Street

Subway station
51st Street (line 6)

Buses
15, 27

Jewish Museum   E3

This museum, run by the Jewish Theological Seminary of America, was founded in 1904 and is now housed in a Renaissance-style mansion (1908), which belonged to the banker Felix M. Warburg, and in a modern annex opened in 1962.
The museum has the world's largest collection of Jewish material, in particular cult objects from synagogues and Jewish establishments in many countries, including Torah scrolls with their gold and silver plates, Sabbath candlesticks, Kiddush cups and jewellery, etc., belonging to the Harry G. Friedman Collection which is housed on the upper floor.
The museum also contains the Benguiat Collection, which includes material ranging in date from medieval to modern times. There are regular special exhibitions of Jewish art and displays on various Jewish themes.

Address
1109 Fifth Avenue
(92nd Street)

Subway station
96th Street (line 6)

Buses
1, 2, 3, 4

Opening times
Mon.–Thurs. noon–5 p.m.,
Sun. 11 a.m.–6 p.m.

*Lincoln Center for the Performing Arts   C5

The construction of the Lincoln Center has not only transformed a whole district of New York but has also provided a model and a stimulus for many other American cities which have developed similar projects.

Situation
Broadway, between 61st
and 66th Streets

Lincoln Center: Metropolitan Opera

Lincoln Center: The New York State Theater

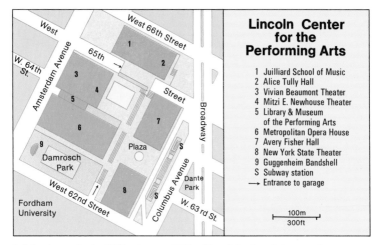

Lincoln Center for the Performing Arts

1 Juilliard School of Music
2 Alice Tully Hall
3 Vivian Beaumont Theater
4 Mitzi E. Newhouse Theater
5 Library & Museum
  of the Performing Arts
6 Metropolitan Opera House
7 Avery Fisher Hall
8 New York State Theater
9 Guggenheim Bandshell
S Subway station
→ Entrance to garage

Building began in the 1950s, the cost (165 million dollars) being met from private sources; the only financial contribution by public authorities was towards the purchase of the site. The individual buildings were designed by different architects, but their neo-classical exterior elevations give them a considerable degree of unity. The material used in all the buildings was Italian travertine, which is resistant to the effects of dust and pollution and does not become discoloured.

Subway stations
66th Street (line 1),
59th Street (lines A, B, D, AA, CC)

Buses
50, 7, 30, 104

Conducted tours
Daily 10 a.m.–5 p.m., starting from Avery Fisher Hall

Individual buildings:

The Avery Fisher Hall, formerly known as the Philharmonic Hall, was the first of the buildings to be finished (1962). It is the home of the New York Philharmonic Orchestra, which gives four concerts weekly from mid September to mid May. Performances by other orchestras and soloists also take place. During the summer a series of concerts lasting several weeks is given under the name "Mostly Mozart" (information: tel. 877 2424). The conducted tours of the Lincoln Center start from the main lobby of the Avery Fisher Hall; the tour lasts about $1\frac{1}{4}$ hours (information: tel. 877 1800).

Avery Fisher Hall

Completed in 1964, this is the home of the New York City Opera Company (tel. 877 4700) and the New York City Ballet Company (see Practical Information, Music).

New York State Theater

The world-famed opera house, the "Met", was opened in 1966. It is the largest building in the Lincoln Center, with seating for 3800.
The Met stands in the centre of the whole complex. It has two large murals by Marc Chagall, which are visible when one enters the building (unless they have been covered for protection from the sun). The interior, as in the other buildings, is in conservative style. For information, tel. 799 3100; also see Practical Information, Music.

Metropolitan Opera House

Little Italy

Alice Tully Hall

This concert hall, designed for chamber music and solo recitals (1100 seats), is on the ground floor of the Juilliard School of Music, New York's largest music academy. Both the hall and the school were opened in 1968.

Every year in early autumn the New York Film Festival is held in the Alice Tully Hall. It is organised by the Lincoln Center Film Society, which has no premises of its own.

Vivian Beaumont Theater

Surely the finest theatre in New York, designed by Eero Saarinen (1100 seats), this was opened in 1968 but has had an unhappy history, having been closed, apart from short periods, since 1978.

The same fate has befallen a small circular theatre with seating for 300, the Mitzi E. Newhouse Theater.

Library and Museum of the Performing Arts

This branch of the New York Public Library contains archive material on the history of the theatre, film, dance and music (open to the public), together with films, recordings, etc.; there is also a lending library. Attached to the Library is the Bruno Walter Auditorium (named after the great German conductor), in which concerts, film shows and lectures are given (usually free of charge). Entrance adjoining the Vivian Beaumont Theater and at 111 Amsterdam Avenue (information: tel. 930 0800).

Lincoln Center Plaza

During the month of August a variety of dramatic and other performances are given (usually at noon, admission free) in the Lincoln Center Plaza, which is laid out round a central fountain.

Little Italy   E/F10

Subway stations
Spring Street (line 6),
Prince Street (line RR)

Immediately NW of Chinatown (see entry) is another of New York's smaller ethnic enclaves, Little Italy, now increasingly losing its identity as a result of the northward movement of the Chinese population. The Little Italy Restoration Association (180 Mott Street, tel. 966 5460) is concerned to preserve the character of this area.

Little Italy, bounded on the S by Canal Street, on the N by Houston Street, on the W by Lafayette Street and on the E by the Bowery, is now mainly occupied by the older Italian American population, since the younger generation has followed the general outward movement to the suburbs. The main N–S streets in Little Italy are Mulberry and Mott Streets, the main E–W streets Grand and Broome Streets.

In Mulberry Street are many Italian restaurants (one of the best known being Paolucci, No. 149, in a building dating from 1816) and Italian-style cafés (the best known of which is Ferrara, established 1892, at 195 Grand Street, around the corner from Mulberry Street). There are also numerous Italian shops and men's clubs in Little Italy.

There were plans to establish a new centre of the Italian quarter in the former police headquarters at 240 Centre Street, a building in the style of a French town hall erected in 1909, but the money required for the conversion could not be found, and at the beginning of 1981 a plan to convert the building into a luxury hotel was announced.

The most interesting time to visit Little Italy is during the second

Street scene in Little Italy

week in September, when there are celebrations for the feast of St Januarius, who is regarded as the patron saint of the quarter (see Practical Information, Events). During this week more than 300 stalls selling a variety of goods and refreshments are set up along both sides of Mulberry Street and the other streets of Little Italy.

Lower East Side   F/G9

One of the more cosmopolitan of Manhattan's ethnic enclaves is Lower East Side, an immense huddle of the apartment blocks in which the great waves of immigrants between 1880 and 1914 found some kind of living accommodation.

In contrast to Harlem (see entry), which was originally a good residential district, Lower East Side was built to house the poorer classes of the population, and apart from one or two modern apartment blocks has retained its original character. At the beginning of the 20th c. this was a purely Jewish area, as witness its 500 or so synagogues and schools, only a few of which still serve their original purpose.

Later the Chinese moved into Lower East Side as they did into Little Italy (see entry), coming from Chatham Square by way of East Broadway; and a new wave of Spanish-speaking immigrants from Puerto Rico and Central and South America moved in from the E. As a result the area has lost the clear identity which it formerly possessed.

The Jewish element is still strongest in Hester, Essex and Rivington Streets and above all in Orchard Street, where there

Subway station
Delancey Street (line F)

Buses
8, 12

are large numbers of fashion, shoe, fur and other shops, many of them displaying and selling their wares on the street.

The area is at its busiest on Sundays (the Jewish shops being closed on Saturdays), with something of the atmosphere of a North African or Near Eastern bazaar. Since prices are low and quality is remarkably high, the Orchard Street shops are patronised by many people from "uptown". The only difficulty of shopping in this area is that customers cannot try things on. There are also many Jewish restaurants in Lower East Side. The most interesting are the Garden Cafeteria (165 East Broadway, corner of Rutgers Street), Katz's Delicatessen (205 East Houston Street) and Bernstein's (135 Essex Street), where Chinese dishes are prepared kosher fashion.

In spite of some efforts that have been made to arrest it, the decline of Lower East Side seems likely to continue.

**Metropolitan Museum of Art   D/E4

Situation
Fifth Avenue and
82nd Street

Subway station
86th Street (lines 4, 5, 6)

Buses
1, 2, 3, 4

Opening times
Tues. 10 a.m.–8.45 p.m.,
Wed.–Sat. 10 a.m.–
4.45 p.m., Sun. 11 a.m.–
4.45 p.m.

Closed
Mon.

Audioguides
(Recorded tours)

The Metropolitan Museum of Art – America's largest museum of art and the third largest in the world, only the British Museum and the Hermitage in Leningrad being larger – was founded in 1870 on the private initiative of a group of New York citizens who believed that their city, with a population then approaching a million, ought to have an art museum of its own. The museum's first home was on West 14th Street, in those days the city centre; soon afterwards it moved to a mansion on Lower Fifth Avenue; and finally the city set aside a site on the E side of the newly created Central Park (see entry) for the building of a new museum. In 1880 Calvert Vaux, who was closely involved in the planning of Central Park, erected a red-brick building which is now visible only from Central Park. The present main building on Fifth Avenue was opened in 1902, the central range being designed by Richard Morris Hunt and Richard Howland Hunt (father and son), the two side wings by McKim, Mead and White. Apart from a number of minor alterations there was no further extension of the building until 1965, when the Thomas J. Watson Library was opened, followed by the Robert Lehman Pavilion (1975), the Sackler Wing, housing the Temple of Dendur (1978), the American Wing (1980) and the Michael C. Rockefeller Wing (1982).

Although the Museum will have more than 300 galleries when the present building programme is complete, it will still be unable to display more than a quarter of its holdings, which increase more rapidly (mainly by gifts) than the space available to show them. Moreover the increasing number of special exhibitions mounted by the "Met" make ever greater demands on display space at the expense of the permanent collection. The Museum's total stock amounts to more than 400,000 items, and even the 100,000 items that are normally on display are far more than any visitor can take in even on repeated visits. The best plan, therefore, is to be selective: make sure that you see what really interests you, and be content with a general impression of the rest.

There are regular conducted tours of the Museum, free of charge (information: tel. 535 7710). Photography (without tripod or flash) is permitted except in the case of special exhibitions, for which special permission is required.

Metropolitan Museum of Art – a bird's-eye view

Going up the broad flight of steps in front of the Museum (on which hundreds of people are glad to rest and enjoy the sunshine during the summer months), we enter the large entrance hall, in which are an information desk, a large museum shop selling reproductions, gifts and books (perhaps the largest selection of art books in New York), cloakrooms (coat check), the ticket office (suggested voluntary admission fee) and a desk at which recorded "Autoguides" can be hired.

To the left of the entrance is the gallery of Greek and Roman art, and beyond this the large Fountain Restaurant (cafeteria). To the right of the entrance is the Egyptian collection, leading to the Temple of Dendur. Also on the Main Floor are the Library (the largest art library in America, with 170,000 volumes and over 1000 periodicals), the collection of arms and armour, medieval art, the Robert Lehman Collection, European sculpture, French and English period rooms (mainly 18th c.) and the entrance to the American Wing.

There are frequent concerts and recitals in the Grace Rainey Rogers Auditorium, which is also on the Main Floor.

The Egyptian collection, one of the largest of its kind in the world, has been substantially enriched by expeditions organised by the Museum in 1930–6 and by the purchase of important private collections. The Temple of Dendur, which was removed from its original site during the construction of the Aswan Dam, was presented by Egypt to the United States and assigned by the US government to the Metropolitan Museum.

In addition to a variety of background material the Egyptian galleries contain reliefs and sculpture of the 1st–10th dynasties

(3100–2040 B.C.); 11th dynasty material from excavations at Thebes; hundreds of coloured facsimiles of tomb and temple paintings of the 3rd millennium B.C.; 30th dynasty material (4th c. B.C.); art of the period of Greek and Roman rule, from Alexander the Great to Cleopatra; and Egyptian art from the early years of the Christian era, showing strong Roman influence, including material from the Fayyum oasis.

The small Gold Room contains gold jewellery, some of it dating from the 19th c. B.C., together with ivory figures and glass.

After a long reconstruction programme the 32 galleries were reopened in the summer of 1983. The collection, now in chronological order, comprises about 10,000 exhibits.

Greek and Roman Art

The collection of Greek and Roman art dates back to the 3rd millennium B.C. with a series of Cycladic idols. There are also numerous works of Cypriot art, brought to New York by the Museum's first director, Luigi di Cesnola, who had been US consul in Nicosia. There are nine galleries on the Main Floor and another eight on the Second Floor.

Among the most notable exhibits are figures of kouroi, marble and stone statues of naked youths (6th c. B.C.), together with grave monuments and everyday objects of the same period; Cycladic statuettes, terracottas, works of Minoan and Mycenaean art; Cypriot stone statues, some of them life-size; Greek vases; gold and silver jewellery; late Roman sarcophagi and portrait sculpture; and mosaics and wall paintings from a villa buried by the eruption of Vesuvius in A.D. 79.

Medieval Art

The Museum's collection of medieval art occupies five galleries, supplemented by the material displayed in the associated museum at the Cloisters (see entry).

Notable features are examples of Byzantine art; Gothic works of art from France; Hispano-Mauresque ceramics; Flemish and Burgundian tapestries; and the Medieval Treasury, containing ivory tablets of the Carolingian and Ottonian periods and French ivories, both sacred and secular.

Gallery 4 is built in the form of a Gothic church, with a nave and aisles. It contains a large collection of Gothic sculpture.

Arms and Armour

Since the United States has no army museum the Met has extended its scope to include arms and armour, and over the years has built up the largest American collection of its kind, displayed in nine galleries surrounding a large Knights' Hall. The exhibits include firearms and other weapons from the bow and arrow to the 19th c. Colt pistol, armour ranging in date from the 14th to the 18th c. and a series of helmets, shields, greaves, etc., made by the best known European armourers (particularly those of Toledo).

Robert Lehman Collection

As a condition of acquiring the private art collection assembled by the banker Robert Lehman (the value of which was estimated at 100 million dollars when it was presented to the Museum some ten years ago) the Met undertook to erect a special building to house it; and an excellently contrived annex was built for this purpose by Kevin Roche and John Dinkeloo, the architects responsible for the other recent extensions to the Museum.

The collection is displayed in seven rooms modelled on those in the former Lehman mansion on West 54th Street and in a

SECOND FLOOR

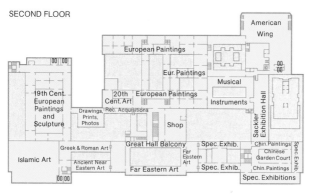

FIRST (MAIN) FLOOR

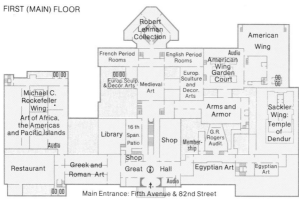

GROUND FLOOR

Metropolitan Museum of Art

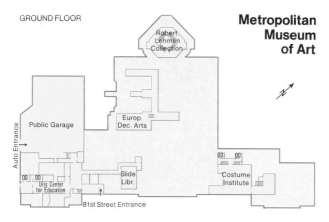

number of other galleries laid out round a glass-roofed courtyard. It includes 300 pictures, over 1000 drawings and numerous other items, and enjoys a virtual independent existence within the Museum, with its own keeper, who is solely responsible for the special exhibitions put on here. The drawings, including works by Leonardo da Vinci, Dürer, Rembrandt and Tiepolo, are displayed on the Ground Floor. Early Italian painting is particularly well represented, and there are also works by El Greco, Rembrandt, Memling, Holbein, Cranach the Elder and 19th and 20th c. painters, particularly Goya, van Gogh, Gauguin, Matisse, Corot, Seurat and Derain. Here, too, is the portrait of the Princesse de Broglie by Ingres, perhaps one of the most celebrated of 19th c. paintings.

American Wing

The American Wing (opened 1980), which covers all aspects of American fine art and applied art, can be reached by way of the Arms and Armour hall or the Temple of Dendur. When finally completed this wing will be able to display the whole of the Museum's collection of American art, and it already has some 14,000 sq. m. (150,000 sq. ft) of display space available in its 63 galleries (40 on the Main Floor and the rest on the Second Floor).

In the centre of this wing is the glass-roofed Engelhard Court, around which have been re-erected the façade (1822–4) of the old United States Bank in Wall Street, a loggia from the villa of Louis Comfort Tiffany with its famous Art Nouveau stained glass, and a staircase (designed by the well-known architect Louis Sullivan) from the old Stock Exchange in Chicago.

Other features of particular interest are 18 furnished rooms (mainly 18th and 19th c.) from different parts of the United States; a selection from the Museum's collection of over 1000 paintings, 1000 watercolours, 125 pieces of sculpture and numerous drawings by American artists (one gallery being devoted exclusively to the work of Winslow Homer); applied art of two centuries, including 850 pieces of silver and 200 of pewter; and a large collection of glass, ceramics and textiles. American architecture will also take an important place in this wing.

Michael C. Rockefeller Wing

This newly furnished imposing addition commemorates the son of Nelson Rockefeller, Michael, who was lost in the Pacific some 20 years ago. The exhibits include African, Latin-American and South-Sea art (primitive art).

Second Floor

On the Second Floor, in addition to the continuation of the American Wing, are European paintings (the central feature of the Museum), Islamic, Far Eastern and Near Eastern art, 20th c. art, the André Meyer Galleries of 19th c. art, prints and drawings and the Museum's collection of musical instruments.

European Paintings

The collection of European paintings of the 14th–18th c. is housed in 34 galleries, arranged in approximate chronological order. The first galleries are devoted to the art of Italy.

Notable among the Italian works are an altarpiece of the Virgin from the convent of Sant'Antonio (1505), Andrea del Sarto's "Holy Family", Tintoretto's "Finding of Moses", "Venus" by Titian and by Paul Veronese, works by Giotto, Taddeo Gaddi and various Sienese painters, Carlo Crivelli's "Virgin and Child", two Virgins by Bellini and paintings by Botticelli, Ghirlandaio, Fra Filippo Lippi, Tiepolo, Guardi, Canaletto, Caravaggio and Guido Reni.

The Metropolitan Museum's special exhibitions are a great draw

Among the Dutch masters pride of place must go to Rembrandt, with no fewer than 33 pictures, including "Aristotle with a Bust of Homer", "Lady with a Pink" and "Man with a Magnifying Glass". Other outstanding items are Vermeer's "Young Woman with a Water-Jug" and works by Frans Hals, Van Dyck, Ruysdael the Elder and Younger, Pieter de Hooch, Gerard ter Borch, Jan Steen, Hendrick Terbrugghen and Jan van Goyen.

Perhaps the finest part of the Museum's collection of French painting (the 19th c. schools) is now to be seen in the new André Meyer Galleries (see below), leaving this section "only" with works by masters of the 15th–17th c. (Georges de la Tour, Nicolas Poussin, Claude Lorrain, etc.) and the great 18th c. painters (Nattier, Watteau, Boucher, Greuze and Fragonard, etc.).

Flemish painters represented include the brothers Jan and Hubert van Eyck, Rogier van der Weyden, Hugo van der Goes, Dieric Bouts, Gerard David, Hans Memling ("Annunciation", "Portrait of an Old Man", "Woman with Carnation"). Then follow, in chronological order, Albrecht Dürer ("Virgin and Child with St Anne"), Hans Holbein the Younger and Lucas Cranach the Elder ("Judgment of Paris", "Martyrdom of St Barbara", portrait of Duke John of Saxony).

Two further galleries contain works by Rubens and his pupils, including a portrait by Van Dyck of James I of England (VI of Scotland).

Many of the Flemish and German pictures came from the collection of the New York businessman Benjamin Altman, as did many of the Museum's Spanish paintings. These include three El Grecos (including one of his most famous works, the view of Toledo in a storm), works by Ribera and Zurbarán and four pictures by Velázquez, including the portrait of Juan de Pareja, the artist's assistant, for which the Museum paid what at the time of its purchase, more than a decade ago, was the highest price ever paid for a painting (5,600,000 dollars).

Another gallery is devoted to British painting, including works by William Hogarth, Reynolds, Raeburn, Gainsborough and Lawrence – all mainly portrait painters.

André Meyer Galleries

These galleries, opened in 1980, display the Museum's collection of 19th c. French art (the boundaries of the period being sufficiently widely drawn to include Jacques-Louis David on the one hand and Henri Rousseau and Bonnard on the other). There are also a number of works by Goya and pictures by Turner, Constable and various minor Italian, German and Russian masters.

The first gallery is devoted to neo-classical and Romantic art, including David's "Death of Socrates" and several portraits by Ingres. The next gallery ("Origins of the 19th Century") contains ten pictures by Goya (the best known perhaps being "The Two Majas on the Balcony"), major works by Delacroix, Constable and Turner, and a picture by the Swiss woman artist Angelica Kauffmann ("Telenachus and Calypso's Nymphs").

The third gallery is devoted to Courbet; its 22 pictures constitute one of the largest assemblages of his work in the world. Then follows a collection of Salon paintings (i.e. mostly pictures exhibited at the annual Salons of the French Royal Academy).

Three small rooms are occupied by works of the Barbizon

Temple of Dendur

school (Millet, Daubigny, Théodore Rousseau, Corot, Daumier). Beyond this is a room containing works by the Symbolists (Puvis de Chavanne, Gustave Moreau, Edward Burne-Jones) and – a little out of place in this company – two portraits by Gustav Klimt.

A long sculpture gallery contains 40 works by Rodin (in bronze, marble, terracotta and plaster) and others by Bourdelle, Maillol and Jules Dalou.

Not surprisingly, the most prominent place is occupied by the Impressionists and Post-Impressionists. There are 18 Manets and no fewer than 29 Monets (though they include none of his greatest works). A recent acquisition is Henri Fantin-Latour's "Still Life with Flowers and Fruit". Van Gogh is represented by two pictures, "Irises" and "L'Arlésienne". There are 17 pictures by Cézanne, works by Renoir, Seurat, Signac and Bonnard, and two important Gauguins.

Returning towards the Rodin gallery, we come to three galleries containing about 100 works by Edgar Degas – one of the largest collections of this artist's work in any museum. They include paintings, pastels and sculpture.

The ten galleries of Islamic art, adjoining the André Meyer Galleries, have recently been reorganised. The exhibits include material dating from the early days of Islam recovered by excavation in Iran; items of the Caliphate period from Spain and Iraq and of the Seljuk period in Iran, Iraq and Turkey; works of the Ayyubid and Mamluk periods (12th–16th c.); characteristic examples of book illumination of the Timurid period in Iran; carpets of the Safavid period in Iran (16th–18th c.) and the Ottoman period in Turkey; and items illustrating the influence of Islamic art in India during the Mogul period (16th–19th c.). In one of the Islamic galleries is the richly decorated living room of an early 18th c. house in Damascus.

Islamic Art

Although the Museum's collection of ancient Near Eastern art is not large it contains a number of choice items. Excavations carried on by the Museum in Iran and Iraq, continuing into quite recent years, have yielded many treasures: thus in south-western Iraq the site of the great city of Lagash (3rd c. B.C.) was excavated, revealing among much else a Babylonian temple and a building of the Sumerian period.

Also of great interest are the ivory tablets and figures from the Assyrian capital, Nimrud. The Museum's collection of Assyrian art has now been brought together in a new Assyrian section opened in 1981.

Ancient Near Eastern Art

The Museum has a considerable collection of Far Eastern art, amounting to over 30,000 items, but can display only a small proportion of the total. One major acquisition was a large collection of jade (1000 items) presented to the Museum at the beginning of the present century. Chinese porcelain and bronzes are well represented (cases on either side of the main staircase). Most of the Museum's Chinese stone sculpture is now housed in the Sackler Gallery: one notable item is a 4 m (12 ft) high figure of a Bodhisattva. Here, too, is a huge Buddhist wall painting (14th c.) from Shansi province.

In comparison with the Chinese material the items from Japan, Korea, India, Nepal and Tibet fall short both in quantity and in quality.

Far Eastern Art

Morris Jumel Mansion

20th Century Art

The Met entered this field only after the last war – undeterred by the fact that here it is in competition with other New York museums. With few exceptions the collection is confined to works by American painters – Max Weber, Joseph Stella, Marsden Hartley, Lyonel Feininger, Arthur Dove, Georgia O'Keefe, Charles Demuth, George Bellows, Edward Hopper, Reginald Marsh, Isobel Bishop, Ben Shann, Andrew Wyeth, Stuart Davis, Arshile Gorky, Jackson Pollock, Willem de Kooning, Franz Kline, Mark Rothko, Adolph Gottlieb, Mark Tobey, Robert Motherwell, Helen Frankenthaler, Ellsworth Kelly, Kenneth Noland, Morris Louis, Barnet Newman, etc. This section also includes 20th c. decorative arts.

Musical Instruments

The greater part of the Museum's collection of musical instruments was the result of a bequest of 3000 instruments from all parts of the world which were left to it by a New York banker's widow at the beginning of the 20th c. This has been supplemented by another 1000 items acquired since then. Among the chief treasures of the collection are three Stradivarius violins, the first pianoforte (1720) and two Flemish double virginals (16th c.).
From time to time the Museum puts on recitals of early music played on instruments of the period.

Costume Institute and
Junior Museum

On the ground floor is the Costume Institute which possesses a large collection of costumes, clothing and accessories; although relatively little is on display, there are always interesting special exhibitions. In the basement is the Ruth and Harold D. Iris Center for Education, opened in 1983, which is intended to introduce visitors, especially young people, to the treasures of the Museum and to art in general.

Morris Jumel Mansion

Situation
160th Street and
Edgecombe Avenue

Subway stations
163rd Street (line AA),
157th Street (line 1)

Opening times
Tues.–Sun. 10 a.m.–4 p.m.

This historic mansion on the northern outskirts of Harlem (see entry) is one of the oldest buildings still standing in Manhattan. It was built by Roger Morris in 1765 and was used by Washington as his headquarters after the American forces withdrew to New York in face of the British advance.

The house contains interesting 18th and 19th c. American furniture and pictures, drawings, silver, china and glass dating from the early days of the United States.

Museo del Barrio   E2

Address
1230 Fifth Avenue

Subway station
103rd Street (line 6)

Buses
1, 2, 3, 4

This museum, founded in 1969, is the only one in the United States exclusively devoted to Puerto Rican and Latin American art. The collection, which is steadily growing, is supplemented by exhibitions of pictures, sculpture and photographs.

The Museum is open Tuesday–Friday 10.30 a.m.–4.30 p.m., Saturday and Sunday 11 a.m.–4 p.m.

Museum of African-American Art

See Studio Museum of Harlem

Museum of American Folk Art   D6

The Museum's collection of predominantly American folk art – including textiles, patchwork quilts and figures of Indians used as tobacconists' signs as well as pictures and sculpture from colonial times to the present day – is displayed in a series of special exhibitions devoted to particular subjects or themes which have attracted considerable interest by their originality. The Museum is open Wednesday–Sunday 10.30 a.m.– 5.30 p.m., Tuesday 10.30 a.m.–8 p.m. Admission is free after 5.30 p.m. on Tuesdays.

Address
47 West 53rd Street

Subway station
53rd Street

Buses
1, 2, 3, 4 (uptown),
6, 7 (downtown)

* Museum of the American Indian

This museum, founded in 1916 by one of Rockefeller's associates, George C. Heye, was originally designed to house only his own collection of Indian artefacts from the American South-West, but was later extended to cover the native cultures of the whole American continent, from the Arctic to Tierra del Fuego. It now possesses one of the largest collections of its kind in America and is the only museum which collects material from the whole of North, Central and South America.

Situation
Broadway and 155th Street

Subway stations
157th Street (line 1),
155th Street (line AA)

Buses
4, 5

Opening times
Tues.–Sat. 10 a.m.–5 p.m.,
Sun. 1–5 p.m.

First Floor
Material from the Eastern and Middle Western United States.

Second Floor
Archaeological material from North America and ethnological material from Alaska, Canada, the North-Western USA, California and the South-West.

Third Floor
Archaeological and ethnological material from the West Indies, Central America and South America.

The museum has a research centre and library in the Bronx devoted to the history and culture of the American Indians. In the middle of 1983 the museum administration resolved to transfer the collection to the American Museum of Natural History (see entry), but it will be several years before the collection will be re-settled.

Museum of Broadcasting   E6

This museum, founded as recently as 1976 but rapidly growing, has what must be America's largest collection of tape recordings, dating back to the Second World War and including many popular programmes. Visitors can listen to the recordings. There is also a collection of over 2000 radio scripts.

Address
1 East 53rd Street

Subway station
Fifth Avenue (lines E, F)

Television films are shown and discussions arranged about radio and television.

Buses
1, 2, 3, 4

The Museum is open Tuesday–Saturday noon–5 p.m.

Museum of the City of New York   E2

Situation
Fifth Avenue and
103rd Street

Subway station
103rd Street (line 6)

Buses
1, 2, 3, 4

Opening times
Tues.–Sat. 10 a.m.–5 p.m.,
Sun. and holidays 1–5 p.m.

Admission free

In spite of its name this museum, like all the other New York museums, is privately run. Founded in 1923, it is concerned with the history of the city, stretching back for more than 300 years.

The Museum was originally housed in the Gracie Mansion (see entry): the present neo-classical building was erected in 1932. It now contains a total of some 500,000 objects and documents, including an extensive archive of material on the history of the theatre and concerts in the city.

First Floor
Dioramas and other exhibits illustrating the early development of New York, from the colonial period to the American revolution.

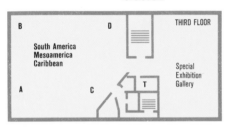

Museum of the American Indian

THIRD FLOOR

A South American Ethnology
B South American Archaeology
C Mesoamerican Archaeology
D West Indies
T Toilets

SECOND FLOOR

A Far West
B Northwest Coast
C Canada
D Eskimo
E Northeast
F Southeast
G Southwest
H Midwest
T Toilets

FIRST FLOOR

1 Main entrance
2 Reception
3 Indian Information Center
4 Museum Shop
A Eastern Woodlands
B Great Lakes
C Plains
D Plateau

Second Floor
Of particular interest are the interiors of New York houses of the 17th–19th c., with life-size figures in contemporary dress.

Third Floor
On this floor is a very large collection of dolls' houses, toy theatres and toys of earlier days. There is also a series of shop-fronts from old New York shops.

Fifth Floor
Reproductions, accurate to the smallest detail, of two rooms from the Rockefeller mansion on West 54th Street, pulled down 30 years ago.

Ground Floor
History of the New York fire brigade and of the national sport of baseball.

Between April and October the Museum organises conducted walks through different parts of Manhattan (see Practical Information, Sightseeing Tours). From October to May there are concerts in the Museum, and from time to time special exhibitions on particular aspects of the city's history.

Museum of Holography

E10

Holography, or laser photography, is one of the newest forms of art, in which laser beams are used to produce three-dimensional images known as holograms. The Museum has a large collection of such items (including prototypes of historical interest), which is supplemented by periodic special exhibitions.
Films on holography are also shown from time to time.
The Museum is open Wednesday–Sunday noon–6 p.m.

Address
11 Mercer Street

Subway station
Canal Street (lines 6, N, RR)

Buses
1, 6

* * Museum of Modern Art

E6

The Museum of Modern Art, founded in 1929, was one of the first museums devoted exclusively to modern art. It defines this term to include artists born after about 1880 (with the exception of Matisse, Monet, Rodin, Rouault and Vuillard) and, with some reservations, young contemporary painters and sculptors.
The Museum was originally housed in an office block at 730 Fifth Avenue (corner of 57th Street), where its first exhibition of 100 pictures by French Impressionists (all loans to the Museum) was held in November 1929. In January 1930 its entire stock consisted of one painting, one piece of sculpture and seven prints; but in the following year it received its first sizeable gift of pictures following the death of Lillian P. Bliss, one of the Museum's founders. Another of its founders, Mrs John D. Rockefeller, donated in the course of her life no fewer than 190 pictures, 137 drawings, 44 works of sculpture and more than 1600 prints by modern artists.
After being accommodated for seven years in a mansion belonging to the Rockefeller family on West 53rd Street, the

Address
18 West 54th Street

Subway station
Fifth Avenue (lines E, F)

Buses
1, 2, 3, 4, 5 (uptown),
6, 7 (downtown)

Opening times
Fri.–Tues. 11 a.m.–6 p.m.,
Thurs. 11 a.m.–9 p.m.

Museum moved into the first section of a new building on the same site (architects Philip Goodwin and Edward Durell Stone) in May 1939. In 1951 an annex designed by Philip Johnson was opened; in 1963 the Museum acquired an adjoining building vacated by the Whitney Museum (see entry) on its move to Madison Avenue; and in 1964 and 1968 further extensions were built. In consequence the complex of buildings occupied by the Museum has a rather heterogeneous aspect.

In the middle of 1983 a 55-storey high skyscraper with 260 private apartments was erected over the museum. After the reconstruction the museum will double its exhibition space. The new museum is due to be finished in 1984. Even then, however – without taking account of its periodic special exhibitions – it will be able to show barely a quarter of its total collection, which in the course of its 50-odd years of existence has risen to almost 4000 pictures and pieces of sculpture, more than 30,000 drawings, prints, photographs, etc., and 4500 films. The annual number of visitors has for several years exceeded a million.

There are daily film shows, almost always forming part of a series, admission to which is included in the ordinary admission ticket. For information about the programme of films telephone 956 7078.

Since the completion of the new "Museum Tower" (in which the Museum will occupy the first eight of the 44 floors) is to be followed by a complete rearrangement of the rooms, it is hardly worth giving a detailed description of the present layout. It seems more useful to give a general account of the scale and scope of the collection.

Museum of Modern Art: a model of the new museum

The Museum's greatest strength probably still lies in the French Impressionists, from Monet to Cézanne. It has four paintings by Monet, and seven paintings and five watercolours by Cézanne (including the famous "Still Life with Apples"). There are also works by Degas, Seurat, Toulouse-Lautrec, Henri (Douanier) Rousseau, Gauguin, Vuillard and Odilon Redon.

French Impressionists

The Museum has one painting and a gouache by Van Gogh.

Van Gogh

Picasso occupies a prominent place in the Museum: indeed for four months in 1980 the Museum was entirely given up to an exhibition of his works (including many on loan from the Picasso Museum in Paris). The permanent collection has (including long-term or permanent loans) almost 70 works by Picasso, including 37 paintings – among them "Les Demoiselles d'Avignon", generally recognised as the first Cubist painting – and numerous bronzes.

Picasso

Georges Braque is represented by nine paintings, Fernand Léger by 22 paintings and half a dozen watercolours, Matisse by some 40 works, including ten paintings and 15 bronzes.

Braque, Léger, Matisse

The 17 pictures by Mondrian, one of the leading members of the Dutch "De Stijl" school, who lived in New York during the Second World War, include a number of his most important works.

Piet Mondrian

The Museum has 11 pictures by Miró.

Joan Miró

Among the Expressionists are Emil Nolde (eight pictures), Kokoschka (seven), Schmitt-Rottluff and Kirchner (four each), Heckel (three) and Otto Müller (one). There is one painting by August Macke and a watercolour by Franz Marc.
Paul Klee is better represented, with 34 works, and there are 12 works by Kandinsky.

German, Austrian and Swiss painters

Max Ernst, Marcel Duchamp and Francis Picabia all spent some time in New York, and the Museum has 21 works by Ernst, 14 by Duchamp and six by Picabia.

Dadaists

Chagall, who also lived in America during the Second World War, is represented by seven paintings and 67 sketches of stage-sets and costumes for the ballet "Aleko".

Marc Chagall

The Museum has works by Giorgio di Chirico, Salvador Dali, Paul Delvaux and René Magritte.

Surrealists

The Abstract Expressionists are the first major American school to be represented in any strength, with works by Adolph Gottlieb, Franz Kline, Robert Motherwell, Ad Reinhardt, James Pollock and Mark Tobey.
All the leading Pop artists including James Dine, Claes Oldenburg, Robert Rauschenberg, Andy Warhol and Tom Wesselman will be found here; but there are few representatives of conceptual art, in which the Museum has so far shown little interest.

American Schools

The Museum has a large collection of modern sculpture, some of it dislayed in a Sculpture Garden (at present closed pending the completion of the Museum Tower). The collection includes

Sculpture

THIRD FLOOR

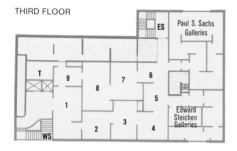

SECOND FLOOR

FIRST FLOOR

11 West 53rd Street

Museum of Modern Art
('MOMA')

SIXTH FLOOR
(not shown)
Penthouse Restaurant
(open noon–3 p.m.)

THIRD FLOOR
1 Picasso after 1930
2 Dadaism
3 Surrealism
4 Surrealism and related schools
5 Post-war European art
6 Abstract Expressionism
7 Abstract Expressionism
8 American and European art of the 1950s
9 American art of the 1950s
Paul S. Sachs Galleries (drawings and prints)
Edward Steichen Galleries (photography)

SECOND FLOOR
1 Post-Impressionism
2 Fantastic art of the end of the 19th c., early Expressionism
3 Analytic Cubism
4 Synthetic Cubism
5 Cubism, Fantastic Cubism
7 The Fauves, Expressionism
10 Futurism
11 Matisse
12 De Stijl, Constructivism, Suprematism
13 "Blauer Reiter", Orphism
14 Ecole de Paris
G Philip L. Goodwin Gallery (architecture and design)

AUDITORIUM LEVEL
(not shown)
Film and video shows

N.B. The Museum is at present undergoing a large-scale extension, during which the *Abby Aldrich Rockefeller Sculpture Garden*, the *René d'Harnoncourt Galleries* and various other parts of the Museum including the Garden Restaurant are closed. After completion of the extension there will be changes in the arrangement of the existing galleries.

☐ Not open to public
☒ Lifts (elevators)

ES East Stairs
WS West Stairs
T Toilets

In the Museum of Modern Art

works by traditional sculptors such as Rodin, as well as by Maillol, Alexander Calder, Jacques Lipchitz, Marino Marini, Henry Moore and Picasso.

The Museum possesses many thousands of drawings, prints, etc., which can be seen, on application, in a special viewing room.

Graphic art

An important element of the Museum is the Edward Steichen Photography Center, named after the famous photographer, a native of Luxembourg, who was the first keeper of the photography department and from whom the Museum received a large proportion of its collection of negatives and original prints.
Since the Museum began collecting photographs in the early thirties, it had a considerable start over other museums.

Edward Steichen
Photography Center

New Museum   E8

In spite of its name this is not a museum but a gallery with no permanent collection.

Address
583 Broadway

Founded in 1977, it puts on periodic exhibitions, mainly of experimental and avant-garde works by young American artists who have still to make a name for themselves.

Subway station
Union Square (line RR)

Opening times are: Thurs., Fri. and Sun. noon–6 p.m., Wed. noon–8 p.m., Sat. 11 a.m.–5 p.m.

Admission free.

* New York Aquarium

Situation
Broadwalk and West 8th
Street, Coney Island,
Brooklyn

Subway stations
West 8th Street (lines D, F),
Stillwell Avenue (line N)

One of the attractions of Coney Island (Brooklyn), New York City's only bathing beach by the sea, is the Aquarium with its large collection of marine fauna. From April to October there are regular performances by trained dolphins, whales and sealions.
The Aquarium is open daily from 10 a.m.–5 p.m.

* New York Botanical Garden

Situation
Bronx Park, Bronx

Subway stations
200th Street/Jerome
Avenue (line 4),
Bedford Park Boulevard
(line D)

Opening times
Daily from 10 a.m.–5 p.m.

The New York Botanical Garden, established in 1891 on the model of the Royal Botanical Gardens at Kew (London), occupies an area of 100 ha (250 acres) at the N end of Bronx Park.
The Conservatory is open daily 10 a.m.–4 p.m. The nearby museum, library, herbarium and research laboratory are a reminder that the gardens serve scientific as well as recreational purposes.
The Bronx River flows through the gardens in a gorge, in which a number of old buildings, including a snuff mill (now a cafeteria), have been preserved.
Admission is free.

New York Experience

See Rockefeller Center

New York Historical Society Museum   D4

Address
170 Central Park West

Subway station
81st Street (lines AA, B, CC)

Bus
10

Opening times
Tues.–Fri. 11 a.m.–5 p.m.,
Sat. 10 a.m.–5 p.m., Sun.
1–5 p.m.

The New York Historical Society, founded in 1809, is one of the city's oldest learned institutions, and its museum is the oldest in New York State. The museum moved to its present site in 1908, but was considerably extended 30 years later.
Among the museum's treasures are 432 of John James Audubon's 1065 watercolours of American birds (near the entrance); a large collection of views of New York from the 17th to the 19th c.; silver by New York silversmiths; domestic interiors of the colonial period; portraits of prominent New Yorkers; popular arts and crafts, and much else. There is also a visual presentation of the city's history from the Dutch colonial period to the end of the 19th c.
The Society's library and photographic archives are essential sources for all students of New York's history.

* New York Public Library   E7

Situation
Fifth Avenue and
42nd Street

The New York Public Library, the largest library in the United States after the Library of Congress in Washington, is – in spite of its name – a private institution, though it now receives more than half its funds from public sources. It was originally formed

New York Public Library

by the amalgamation of three private libraries (the Astor library, established by John Jacob Astor in 1849, and the Lenox and Tilden libraries), and the imposing building of Vermont marble in which it is housed was erected between 1897 and 1911 to the design of the New York architects Carrère and Hastings, half the cost of building it being met by the Scottish-born steel magnate Andrew Carnegie. The site had previously been occupied by a reservoir, which supplied New York with water, and, in the city's early days, a paupers' cemetery.

The main entrance to the Library, a typical example of the "Beaux Arts" school of architecture, is on Fifth Avenue. There are regular exhibitions of material from the Library's collection in the entrance hall, the corridors and Room 318.

On the second floor are various special departments (Slavonic, Jewish, economic and social sciences, etc.), on the third the large Reading Room with seating for 550 readers. Here, too, is the catalogue of the library's total stock of over 5 million volumes, any one of which can be brought from the book-stacks within a matter of minutes from the presentation of an application slip. Also in the Reading Room is a reference library of some 40,000 volumes, including telephone directories for the whole of the United States.

On the same floor are manuscripts (the Berg Collection) and rare books, which can be consulted only by special arrangement.

On the ground-floor level (entrance on 42nd Street) are a lending library and children's library.

The New York Public Library has over 80 branch libraries in Manhattan, the Bronx and Staten Island (Brooklyn and Queens

Subway stations
42nd Street (lines B, D, F),
Fifth Avenue (line 7)

Buses
1, 2, 3, 4, 5, 106

Opening times
Mon.–Sat. 10 a.m.–6 p.m.

Admission free

Conducted tours
Mon., Tues. and Wed. at
11 a.m. and 2 p.m.
(Astor Hall entrance)

Branch libraries

have their own library service and central library). Among these are:

The Mid-Manhattan Library at 8 East 40th Street, a reference library of over 400,000 volumes.

The Donnell Library Center at 20 West 53rd Street, mainly an art, film and video library.

The Library of the Performing Arts in the Lincoln Center (see entry), a reference and lending library in the fields of theatre, film, music and the dance.

The Schomburg Center for Research in Black Culture (see entry).

---

*New York Stock Exchange E11

Address
20 Broad Street

Subway stations
Wall Street (lines 1, 2, 3),
Rector Street (line RR),
Fulton Street (line A)

Opening times
Mon.–Fri. 10 a.m.–4 p.m.

The New York Stock Exchange is the largest in the United States, trading in more than 4400 different stocks and shares. On the Visitors' Balcony, which affords a good view of the circular trading floor, there is a small exhibition (with film shows) explaining the mysteries of trading on the Stock Exchange.

The building, with its façade in the style of a Roman temple, was designed by George B. Post and built in 1903.

The New York Stock Exchange is only one of New York's numerous financial and commercial exchanges. Among the others are the American Stock Exchange at 86 Trinity Place and the Coffee, Sugar and Cocoa Exchange in the World Trade Center (see entry).

New York Stock Exchange

View from Visitors' Balcony

Old Merchant's House   E9

This early 19th c. house, one of the few buildings of the period
to be preserved in its original state, was built by a well-to-do
businessman named Seabury Tredwell in 1832 in what was
then one of New York's most fashionable residential areas.
Nowadays, however, this area between Lafayette Street and
the Bowery (see entry) has deteriorated.

The original furniture of the house has been preserved, and
visitors are shown clothes belonging to Tredwell's daughter
Gertrude, who died in 1933 at the age of 93.

The house was reopened in December 1980 after complete
restoration.

Old Merchant's House is open to the public (by prior telephone
appointment) on Wednesdays and Sundays.

Address
29 East 4th Street

Subway station
Astor Place (line 6)

Buses
1, 5, 6, 101, 102

*Pierpont Morgan Library   E7

The Pierpont Morgan Library is much more than a library: it is
a museum of art and bibliographical treasures assembled from
1890 onwards by the banker J. Pierpont Morgan and his son.
The Library is housed in a Renaissance-style palazzo built for
the elder Morgan in 1903–6 by the well-known firm of New
York architects McKim, Mead and White, with an extension
added in 1928.

Morgan senior accumulated an extraordinary hoard of treasures, first acquiring individual items such as a Gutenberg
Bible, four First Folios of Shakespeare and manuscripts of
Byron, Keats and Dickens, then whole libraries, incunabula,
books printed by Caxton (the first English printer), papyrus
rolls from Egypt, Assyrian cuneiform tablets and much else.

The only manuscripts on public display are those shown in
cases to the left of the Reading Room. The Reading Room can
be used only by scholars and students who are accredited for
the purpose: a four-page leaflet sets out the strict conditions on
which material is made available for study.

There is an Exhibition Hall in which there is always (except
during the summer) a superb display of material from the
Library's own resources or of items loaned for the purpose.

In the long corridor leading to the galleries are prints and
drawings, together with some magnificent examples of French
bookbinding.

Address
29 East 36th Street

Subway station
33rd Street (line 6)

Buses
1, 2, 3, 4

Opening times
Tues.–Sat. 10.30 a.m.–
5 p.m., Sun. 1–5 p.m.

Closed
Sun. in July;
whole of August

Poe Cottage

This little wooden house, built in 1812, was the last home of
Edgar Allan Poe, the first American writer to achieve world
fame. Anxious to get away from crowded Manhattan, Poe
rented the house, then situated in the village of Fordham, in
1846 for 100 dollars a year. Soon afterwards his wife died of
tuberculosis, and in 1849 Poe himself, a notorious alcoholic,
died on his way back from a lecture tour in the South.

In 1902 Poe Park was laid out, and the cottage was moved
across the road to its present site in the park. The interior has

Situation
Grand Concourse and East
Kingsbridge Road (Bronx)

Subway station
Kingsbridge Road
(lines 4, D)

Buses
Bx1, Bx2, Bx4, Bx15, Bx20

Opening times
Mon., Thurs., Fri. and Sun.
1–5 p.m., Sat. 10 a.m.–4 p.m.

been faithfully restored to its original state. Here Poe wrote some of his best known poems, including "Annabel Lee", "Ul■lume" and "Eureka"

P.S.1 (Institute for Art and Urban Resources)

Address
46–01 21st Street
Long Island City (Queens)

Subway stations
Hunter's Point (line 7),
23rd Street/Ely Avenue
(lines E, F)

Opening times
Thurs.–Sun. 1–6 p.m.

"P.S.1" stands for Public School 1, an old elementary school dating from 1890 which stood empty for many years before being leased by the city for a token rent to the Institute for Art and Urban Resources. Since 1975 the former classrooms have been used as studios for artists, who are thus provided with a cheap place to work (though not to live).

P.S.1 puts on a full programme of exhibitions, in which displays of "Minimal" art predominate. It also provides a setting, particularly at weekends, for a variety of performances and 'happenings'. Thus in the course of a very few years this disused school building has developed into an international centre of creative artistic activity.

Public Library

See New York Public Library

* Richmondtown Restoration/ Staten Island Historical Museum

Address
441 Clarke Avenue
(Staten Island)

Boat
Staten Island ferry from
Battery Park, then bus R113

Opening times
From 1 May, Sat. and Sun.
noon–5 p.m.

In the district of Richmondtown, the old centre of Staten Island, 39 houses dating back to 1695 have been carefully restored and now give visitors a vivid impression of life in the colonial period. The oldest of the houses is the Voorlezer's House, with a single room, which is the oldest surviving schoolhouse in America. Other buildings include shops, a printing office, churches, a courthouse and dwelling-houses. The interiors of some of them are open to visitors.

The Staten Island Historical Museum, part of this complex, is housed in a more recent building (1848), originally a government office. It contains a variety of American memorabilia. Here, too, can be obtained a plan of the Richmondtown Restoration, showing which of the 39 houses are open to visitors.

* Rockefeller Center   D/E6

Situation
Fifth Avenue,
48th–51st Streets,
Avenue of the Americas,
47th–52nd Streets

The Rockefeller Center, a complex of 21 high-rise office blocks on Fifth Avenue (48th–51st Streets) and Avenue of the Americas (47th–52nd Streets) is the largest comprehensively planned skyscraper city in the world, a development which has

Rockefeller Center: an unusual angle, with statue of Prometheus

transformed the face of Manhattan over the past 50 years. The initiative for its construction came from America's wealthiest citizen, John D. Rockefeller Jr (to whom New York also owes Rockefeller University, Fort Tryon Park and the Cloisters (see entry), the United Nations Headquarters Building (see entry), for which he provided the site, and Riverside Church).

The Center, built on land belonging to Columbia University, originally consisted of 14 tower blocks between Fifth Avenue and the Avenue of the Americas and between 48th and 51st Streets, but further development from 1954 onwards took it beyond these limits.

In addition to countless offices with a working population of a quarter of a million, the Rockefeller Center contains 30 restaurants, including the famous Rainbow Room on the 65th floor of the RCA Building; dozens of shops on ground-floor level and in the underground passages; television studios, several exhibition halls and the Radio City Music Hall Entertainment Center; a constantly changing flower show from April to November; and a whole museum of mural paintings, sculpture and reliefs (over 100 works of art by more than two dozen artists).

Architecturally most of the buildings are of little interest; but the whole complex as developed between 1931 and 1974 has the great merit that the planners did not cover the whole site with buildings but left a reasonable area of open space.

There are conducted tours of the Center, beginning in the entrance hall of the RCA Building and ending on the Observation Roof on its 69th floor. (Visitors are also allowed to go up to the Observation Roof on their own.)

Subway station
50th Street (lines B, D, F)

Buses
5, 6, 7 (uptown, Avenue of the Americas), 1, 2, 3, 4, 5 (downtown, Fifth Avenue)

Opening times
Tower: Oct.–Mar., daily 10.30 a.m.–7 p.m.,
Apr.–Sept., 10 a.m.–9 p.m.

Conducted tours
Rockefeller Center:
Mon.–Sat. 9.45 a.m.–
4.45 p.m. (every 30 minutes;
RCA Building entrance)

The New York Experience

Address
1221 Avenue of the
Americas

Subway station
50th Street (lines B, D, F)

Buses
5, 7 (downtown), 27

This "multisensory theater" is a new-style cinema with 45 projectors, 16 screens and quadraphonic sound which presents New York in 3D, with full sound effects. The spectators sit on swivelling seats so that they can follow the action taking place all over the auditorium.

On the way in, spectators pass through "Little Old New York", a re-creation of the city at the turn of the century.

The New York Experience is open until midnight.

St Bartholomew's Protestant Episcopal Church   E6

Address
109 East 50th Street

Subway stations
51st Street (line 6),
Lexington Avenue
(lines E, F)

Opening times
Daily until dusk

This church, occupying the block between 50th and 51st Streets, was built by Bertram Goodhue in 1919. It is in an eclectic Byzantine style, with a Romanesque doorway (by McKim, Mead and White) modelled on that of St-Gilles in Arles which came from the previous church at the corner of Madison Avenue and 44th Street. The Byzantine-style interior has an altar by Lee Larrie (best known for his sculpture in the Rockefeller Center).

The future of this ornate church, a little out of place among the surrounding skyscrapers, is in doubt. In 1981 negotiations were in progress for the sale of the site, for a reported 100 million dollars, to a large corporation which proposed to build an office block on the site.

St Mark's in the Bowery   F9

Situation
Second Avenue and
10th Street

Subway station
Astor Place (line 6)

Bus
15

Opening times
Daily until dusk

This is New York's second oldest church, built in 1799 on the site of an earlier chapel erected by Peter Stuyvesant, Dutch governor of New York, on his farm. Stuyvesant and his family are buried in the crypt. Thirty years later a neo-classical tower was added to the colonial-style church, and 26 years after that a Romanesque portico with cast-iron railings.

The church was devastated by fire in 1978 but was reopened in 1981 after restoration (mainly by volunteer helpers).

St Mark's (which is Episcopalian) achieved some prominence in the heyday of the hippie movement, the main centre of which was St Mark's Place, only two blocks away. In 1965 the Genesis Theater, which stages only plays by young US writers, was opened in the church.

*St Patrick's Cathedral   E6

Situation
Fifth Avenue,
between 50th and 51st
Streets

Subway station
Fifth Avenue (lines D, F)

This Roman Catholic cathedral, seat of the Archbishop of New York, was designed by James Renwick in High-Gothic style and built of light-coloured marble between 1858 and 1888. It has two towers with spires rising to a height of 100 m (330 ft). The Lady Chapel at the E end was added in 1901–5.

The Cathedral was dedicated to St Patrick in 1910. The dignified interior is 93 m (305 ft) long and 38 m (125 ft) wide across the transept. It can seat a congregation of 2500.

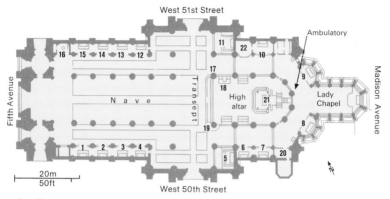

West 51st Street

West 50th Street

20m
50ft

St Patrick's Cathedral

ALTARS
1 St Anthony of Padua
2 St John the Evangelist
3 St Elizabeth Ann Seton
4 St Rose of Lima
5 Sacred Heart
6 St Andrew
7 St Teresa of the Infant Jesus

8 St Elizabeth
9 St Michael and St Louis
10 St Joseph
11 Holy Family
12 Holy Relics
13 St Augustine
14 St John Baptist de la Salle
15 St Brigid and St Bernard

16 Baptistery
17 Statue of St Patrick
18 Archbishop's Throne
19 Pulpit
20 Archbishop's Sacristy
21 Entrance to crypt and
   sacristies
22 Organ

The vaulting is borne on massive marble columns. Notable features of the interior are the stained glass, the canopied High Altar (dedicated 1942), the numerous side altars and the effigy of St Elizabeth Ann Seton (1774–1821), foundress of the order of the Sisters of Charity, who became the first woman saint of the United States in 1975.
The Cathedral's organ has more than 9000 pipes.

Buses
1, 2, 3, 4

Opening times
Daily 6.30 a.m.–8 p.m.

St Paul's Chapel   E11

Built in 1764–6, this is the oldest church in Manhattan; and, unlike other buildings of the period (e.g. see Fraunces Tavern), it has remained substantially unchanged. It was designed by the Scottish architect Thomas McBean and was probably modelled on St Martin-in-the-Fields in London (designed by James Gibb, with whom McBean may have worked as a pupil). The spire and portico were added in 1796.
In the N aisle is George Washington's private pew. The little churchyard attracts many people, particularly in spring and autumn, to enjoy this oasis of peace.

Situation
Broadway and Fulton Street

Subway stations
Fulton Street (lines 4, 5),
Broadway-Nassau (line A)

Opening times
Daily 7 a.m.–4 p.m.

*Schomburg Center for Research in Black Culture

With the opening of its new premises in a five-storey building in Harlem (see entry) in 1980 the Schomburg Center for Research in Black Culture, founded in 1925 as a branch of the

Address
515 Lenox Avenue

Schomburg Center for Research in Black Culture

Subway station
135th Street
(lines 2, 3, AA, BB)

Buses
1, 2A, 101A

Opening times
Mon.–Wed. noon–8 p.m.,
Thurs.–Sat. 10 a.m.–6 p.m.

New York Public Library (see entry) and now the largest establishment of its kind in the world, has at last found a worthy home.

The nucleus of the Schomburg Center was the collection of 5000 books, 300 manuscripts, 2000 etchings and portraits and much other material assembled by Arthur A. Schomburg, a Puerto Rican banker living in New York. From 1932 until his death in 1938 Schomburg himself was the keeper of the collection.

The collection has now grown to over 80,000 volumes, over 200,000 manuscripts, 3000 prints and posters, 15,000 microfilms and 50,000 photographs. The Center also possesses a large store of material on the history, culture and folk traditions of the West Indies, records of African folk music and works of art by African painters and sculptors.

A visit to the Center will be a rewarding experience for anyone interested in the culture of black Africa.

The building itself, with an octagon at one end and a tower at the corner of 135th Street, can be seen as a symbol of the gradual rehabilitation of Harlem.

The tables, chairs and desks in the reading rooms and archive rooms are mostly made of African timber.

Sculpture in New York

In addition to the older monuments and statues there are numerous examples of modern sculpture in Manhattan.

Financial District:
Isamo Noguchi's
"Cube"

Chase Manhattan Plaza:
Jean Dubuffet's
"Four Trees"

Park Avenue:
Louise Nevelson's
"Night Presence IV"

At 140 Broadway is Isamo Noguchi's "Cube" (1973), 7m (23 ft) high.

Financial District

In front of the Police Headquarters is Bernard Rosenthal's "Five in One" (1974). The five interlocking discs represent New York's five boroughs.

Police Plaza

Jean Dubuffet's "Four Trees' (1972), a monumental piece of sculpture 14 m (46 ft) high and weighing 25 tons which Dubuffet described as "a monument to the spirit, a landscape of the mind".

Chase Manhattan Plaza

Rudolph de Harak's "Helix" (1969), a spiral of stainless steel 7 m (22 ft) high, and William Tarr's "Rejected Skin" (1971), a piece of abstract sculpture made from rejected aluminium left over from the construction of a building.

77 Water Street

Yu Yu Yang's "Queen Elizabeth I Memorial" (1974), two stainless-steel units commemorating the liner, not the queen.

Wall Street Plaza

In Astor Place is Bernard Rosenthal's "Alamo" (1967), the first work of modern sculpture set up in a New York Street.
At 100 Bleecker Street is the "Bust of Sylvette", designed by Picasso and executed by the Norwegian sculptor Carl Nesjar (1968). This piece of concrete sculpture, weighing 60 tons, stands four storeys high, in front of the New York University

East Village

residences. In spite of its great size this sphinx-like figure has a curious grace.

Avenue of the Americas

At No. 1221 is Athelstan Spilhaus's "Sun Triangle" (1973). Various parts of this modern sun-dial of stainless steel point to the position of the sun at noon at the solstices and equinoxes. At No. 1271 is William Crovello's "Cubed Curve" (1971). The steel curves, painted blue, of this piece of sculpture form an effective counterpoint to the straight lines of the Time-Life Building behind it.

Central Park

At the Fifth Avenue/60th Street entrance to Central Park (see entry) is Louise Nevelson's "Frozen Laces – One" (1979–80), 10 m (33 ft) high, and made of painted stone.

Lincoln Center

In front of the Library and Museum of the Performing Arts is Alexander Calder's "Le Guichet" ("The Ticket Window", 1972), a typical Calder "stabile" of blackened steel.
Outside the Vivian Beaumont Theatre is Henry Moore's "Reclining Figure" (1968), a two-part work of sculpture in blackened bronze, reflected in the water of the pool in which it stands. It is illuminated after dark.

Park Avenue

At 92nd Street is Louise Nevelson's "Night Presence IV" (1972), 7 m (22 ft) high, made of steel alloyed with nickel and copper, which are gradually giving it a brownish-black hue.

Skyscrapers

The real architectural history of New York begins towards the end of the 19th c., when the development of the elevator made it possible to erect buildings higher than the usual five storeys. Until then New York architects had developed little originality of their own, being content for the most part to imitate or modify what was being done in Europe. The influence of Britain, France and Italy was ubiquitous.
Elements of the skyscraper style can be identified as early as the mid 19th c., but it was only in the closing years of the century that it took on a distinctive character of its own. Buildings were now erected in accordance with a tripartite principle of composition comparable with the base, shaft and capital of a classical Greek column. Examples of this style are the Metropolitan Life Building and the Flatiron Building.
Soon these were followed by taller skyscrapers with organically designed towers (e.g. the Woolworth Building). Subsequent new building regulations required successive stages to be stepped back, as in the Empire State Building (see entry), the Chrysler Building (see entry) and many others of the late twenties. The next phase, which still holds the field, provided for areas of open space around the buildings (gardens, fountains, seats, etc.) or within them, in the form of an atrium. This trend began with the Rockefeller Center (see entry) in 1930.

Metropolitan Life Building
1 Madison Avenue

Built in 1893 by Napoleon LeBrun (23 and 25 floors). The tower was added 16 years later, which made it the highest building in the world (213 m – 700 ft) for two years.

Flatiron Building

Grace Building

PanAm Building

Skyscrapers

Flatiron Building,
Fifth Avenue and 23rd Street

Built in 1902 by D. H. Burnham. The diagonal alignment of Broadway made it necessary, as at Times Square (see entry), to erect a triangular building with an acutely angled apex, making it look even narrower in perspective.

Woolworth Building,
233 Broadway

Built in 1913 by Cass Gilbert, this was the highest building in the world (241 m – 790 ft) until the completion of the Chrysler Building (see entry) some 17 years later. The architectural critic Paul Goldberger called it "the Mozart among skyscrapers". The Gothic detailing is well adapted to the vertical form of the building, and the tower stretches naturally and organically up from the base. The three-storey lobby is also of notable quality.

Seagram Building,
375 Park Avenue
(53rd Street)

Built in 1958 by Mies van der Rohe and Philip Johnson. It shows the form, later so popular, of a glass-walled skyscraper with a plaza, though the layout of the plaza later became much more interesting.

Chase Manhattan Bank,
1 Chase Manhattan Plaza

Built in 1960 by Skidmore, Owings and Merrill. Situated near Wall Street (see entry), this building marked the beginning of the modernising process of the Financial District. Notable features are the sunken plaza wiuth fountains (by Isamo Noguchi) and a sensational piece of sculpture by Jean Dubuffet.

PanAm Building,
200 Park Avenue
(48th Street)

Built in 1963 by Emery Roth and Sons, Pietro Belluschi and Walter Gropius. Its construction gave rise to fierce criticism, since it blocked the previously open view of Park Avenue. The building, which PanAm sold to an insurance corporation in 1980 for 400 million dollars, can also be entered from Grand Central Station. In the large lobby are works of art by Josef Albers, Gyorgy Kepes and Richard Lippold.

General Motors Building,
767 Fifth Avenue (between
58th and 59th Streets)

Built in 1968, on a site previously occupied by the Savoy Plaza Hotel, by Emery Roth and Sons in collaboration with Edward Durell Stone. Destroying as it does the harmony of Grand Army Plaza, it can be cited as an example of how not to build a skyscraper.

Gulf and Western Building,
Columbus Circle, between
Central Park West and
Broadway

Built in 1969 by Thomas E. Stanley. This is another skyscraper built without regard to its immediate surroundings and which disfigures the skyline of western Manhattan.

W. R. Grace Building,
1114 Avenue of the
Americas and
41 West 42nd Street

Built in 1974 by Skidmore, Owings and Merrill, who, as in another of their buildings at 9 West 57th Street, sought to achieve the setting-back of the upper floors by adopting a curved form.

Olympic Tower,
645 Fifth Avenue
(51st Street)

Built in 1976 by Skidmore, Owings and Merrill. This was the first skyscraper to combine shops, offices and owner-occupied apartments in the same building. The public arcade within the building, however, has failed to achieve the intended effect of lively activity.

Citicorp Building,
Lexington Avenue (between
53rd and 54th Streets)

Built in 1978 by Hugh Stubbins, this was the most discussed building of the 1970s. In addition to shops and restaurants it also incorporates a church (St Peter's, Lutheran) designed by the same architect. The sloping tower of this building, the fifth tallest in Manhattan, is visible from many parts of the city. It was originally planned to use solar energy for the heating of the building, but the structure proved insufficiently strong to support the installation.

This building, completed in 1983 to the design of Edward Larrabee Barnes, stands at the corner of 57th Street and is an important addition to the skyscraper landscape of New York. Built of dark green granite it stands 43 storeys high, with a further four storeys of glassed-in garden (used for concerts etc.) and an exhibition hall for IBM products.

IBM Tower
Madison Avenue

Between 55th and 56th Streets, Philip Johnson, once the enthusiastic champion in America of Mies van der Rohes, has created an "old-fashioned" skyscraper about 195 m (640 ft) high. In designing the building, which was completed in 1983, he has gone back to the classic beginnings of skyscraper architecture. The gabled roof and the six-storeys-high entrance of the pinkish-grey granite building are among its most controversial features.

A.T. & T.
Madison Avenue

The 68 storeys-high skyscraper at the corner of 56th Street was built in 1983 on the site of the fashion-house Bonwit Teller by Scutt and Swanke, Hayden Connell and Partners. Especially noteworthy is the six-storeys-high Atrium, the colour of which can best be described as a mixture of pink, orange and peach, with many luxury shops; above these are offices and private apartments.

Trump Tower
725 Fifth Avenue

The 55-storeys-high skyscraper erected over the Museum of Modern Art is the work of the Argentinian architect, Cesare Pelli. It houses not only additional exhibition rooms for the museum, but also 260 private apartments.

Museum Tower
West 53rd Street

---

*SoHo

The name of this Manhattan district has nothing to do with Soho in London: it is an acronym for So(uth) of Ho(uston Street). This area of about a square mile is bounded on the N by Houston Street, on the W by West Broadway (SoHo's main street), on the S by Canal Street and on the E by Broadway. Some 12 or 15 years ago it was a quiet backwater of warehouses and small factories, but today it is New York's liveliest artists' quarter. It all began when artists took to renting the large areas of space available in disused warehouses and converting them into studios and living accommodation. In the course of time they were followed by numerous galleries, smart shops, restaurants and jazz and rock clubs, and SoHo became a tourist Mecca. Nowadays it hums with life and activity, particularly on Saturday afternoons, except during the quiet summer months.

Subway stations
Spring Street (line AA),
Bleecker Street (line 6)

Nowhere else in America is there such a concentration of 100-year-old cast-iron buildings as can be seen in SoHo (off West Broadway, particularly in Greene Street but also in Broome Street). The use of cast-iron made it possible to produce at low cost columns, arches, doorways and other constructional elements – indeed entire façades – the first use of standardised and prefabricated elements in building. This

SoHo: the artist John De Andrea

gave rise to an abundance of interesting detail which can still be admired. Fifteen years ago a proposal was put forward to demolish almost all the old buildings in this quarter to make way for a new road, but fortunately the plan was frustrated at the eleventh hour and the whole of SoHo is now under statutory protection as a national monument.

A stroll through SoHo is an experience not to be missed. Here you can see the very latest trends in American art and will encounter a seemingly endless range of galleries, boutiques and other interesting shops, restaurants and places of entertainment (see Practical Information, Galleries).

Songwriters Hall of Fame   D6

Address
1 Times Square

Subway station
Times Square
(lines 1, 2, 3, 7, N, RR)

This museum of American light music was opened in 1977 in the old Times Building. It contains a collection of photographs, musical scores, autographs, pianos and other instruments once played by leading composers, theatre programmes, posters, caricatures, etc.
The Hall of Fame is open Monday–Saturday 11 a.m.–3 p.m. Admission free.

*South Street Seaport Museum   F11

Address
16 Fulton Street

The South Street Seaport Museum, established in 1967 as part of a plan to rehabilitate the old port area, lies on East River, to

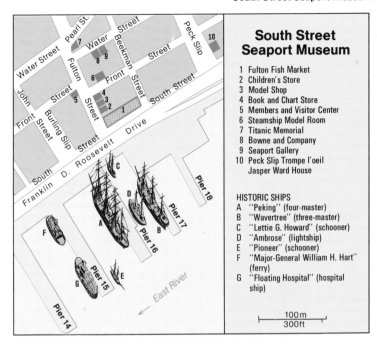

South Street Seaport Museum

1 Fulton Fish Market
2 Children's Store
3 Model Shop
4 Book and Chart Store
5 Members and Visitor Center
6 Steamship Model Room
7 Titanic Memorial
8 Bowne and Company
9 Seaport Gallery
10 Peck Slip Trompe l'oeil
   Jasper Ward House

HISTORIC SHIPS
A "Peking" (four-master)
B "Wavertree" (three-master)
C "Lettie G. Howard" (schooner)
D "Ambrose" (lightship)
E "Pioneer" (schooner)
F "Major-General William H. Hart" (ferry)
G "Floating Hospital" (hospital ship)

100m
300ft

the S of Brooklyn Bridge (see entry). Its scope is wider than its name implies, for it is not only a museum of shipping and the seaport but also contains interesting material on New York in the late 18th and early 19th c.

This was once the centre of New York's port area, and the surviving or restored buildings to be seen here bear witness to the early years of the overseas trade which was the basis of the city's growth and prosperity. In the 1860s, however, when sail gave place to steam, the main port activity moved to the Hudson River, where there was room for the construction of large piers.

The Museum occupies a number of different buildings:

A series of exhibitions on various aspects of seafaring in the past.

Visitors' Information Centre and shop.

Reconstruction of a 19th c. printing office. Lectures are also given here.

Ship models and posters.

At Piers 15 and 16 are moored a number of historic vessels, which are open to visitors. Among them are:

Subway station
Fulton Street
(lines 4, 5, A, CC, J, M)

Bus
15

Opening times
Daily 11 a.m.–6 p.m.

215 Water Street

16 Fulton Street

211 Water Street

203 Front Street

Piers 15 and 16

101

South Street Seaport Museum

The four-master "Peking", built at Hamburg in 1911, which originally shipped guano from Chile to Europe and later became a training ship in Britain.

The "Ambrose" (1907), a lightship.

The "Pioneer" (1885), which is used for three-hour cruises around the port in summer (information: tel. 766 9076).

The "Wavertree", which also dates from 1885.

The "Major-General William H. Hart", once a ferry between Manhattan and Governor's Island, now occupied by the Pioneer Marine School, a school of seamanship.

Fulton Market

The new Fulton Market, opened in 1983, is exclusively for food and eating; in 1984 the Pier 17 Pavilion (shops and restaurants) is expected to open.

** Statue of Liberty and American Museum of Immigration

Situation
Liberty Island

Boat
Ferry from Battery Park
(from 9 a.m. hourly, on the hour; more frequently in summer; for information tel. 269 5755)

The Statue of Liberty, a gift from the French people to the United States, was designed by the Alsatian sculptor Frédéric-Auguste Bartholdi and set up in 1886 on Bedloe's Island (now Liberty Island) at the entrance to the port of New York, where it was the first object to greet immigrants and visitors sailing to the New World. It thus became a symbol of the American ideal, visited over the years by more than 50 million people.

The statue 46 m (151 ft) high and weighing 225 tons, stands on a base 47 m (154 ft) high. There is a staircase of 167 steps inside the base, but most visitors will prefer the elevator (charge ten cents). A spiral staircase of 171 steps – the equivalent of 12

Liberty Island, with the Statue of Liberty

storeys – goes up inside the statue itself: visitors require, therefore, to be in good physical condition.

Informative material about the Statue of Liberty can be obtained in the main lobby.

At the base of the statue is the American Museum of Immigration.

Opening times
Daily 9 a.m. to 5 or 6 p.m.
(restoration work from late 1983)

Admission free

American Museum of Immigration

The idea of establishing a museum of immigration was first put forward in 1954, the foundation stone was laid eight years later and the museum was opened in 1972.

In addition to its permanent display of drawings, photographs, models and audio-visual presentations illustrating the different stages of the immigration movement, the Museum puts on special exhibitions on various aspects of the history of immigration. It covers the whole range from the first Indians who moved into the American continent from Asia to the immigrants of many nationalities and adherents of persecuted religious groups who came into the United States in the 19th and 20th c. A special exhibition is devoted to the large group of immigrants who were brought in against their will – the negroes who were shipped to America from Africa as slaves.

Opening times
Daily 9.15 a.m.–5 p.m.

Admission free

Studio Museum of Harlem   E1

This museum, founded in 1970, is the only museum exclusively devoted to work by contemporary black artists. It has no

Address
144 West 125th Street

Subway station
125th Street
(lines 2, 3, 4, 5, 6)

Opening times
Wed. and Fri. 10 a.m.–
5 p.m., Sat. and Sun.
1–6 p.m., Thurs. 10 a.m.–
9 p.m.

permanent collection but puts on periodic special exhibitions, often including work by Harlem artists. It also serves as a cultural centre for black artists in all fields: the museum itself is on the ground floor of a two-storey building, the upper floor of which has been converted into a large studio for the use of the black community.

Admission free. (For information tel. 864 4500.)

Theodore Roosevelt Birthplace E8

Address
28 East 20th Street

Subway station
23rd Street (lines 6, RR)

Opening times
Wed.–Sun. 9 a.m.–5 p.m.

Closed
Mon. and Tues.,
Oct.–15 May

This house, between Broadway and Park Avenue South, is not the actual house, built in 1848, in which Theodore Roosevelt, 26th President of the United States and the only President born in New York, came into the world in 1858. The original house was destroyed, probably during Roosevelt's lifetime, and four years after his death was rebuilt in its earlier form. The interior has been decorated and furnished as it was in Roosevelt's early days.

Theodore Roosevelt is also commemorated by an equestrian statue (by James Earle Fraser) in front of the American Museum of Natural History (see entry).

*Times Square D6

Subway station
Times Square
(lines 1, 2, 3, 7, N, RR)

Buses
104, 106

Times Square, like some other "squares" in New York, is not really a square at all but the point of intersection of two streets – in this case Broadway and Seventh Avenue.

Known until 1904 as Longacre Square, it was then renamed Times Square after the "New York Times", whose offices were at 1 Times Square (they are now around the corner at 229 West 43rd Street).

The first theatres were built here in 1893, soon to be followed by fashionable restaurants, and from the beginning of the 20th c. this became New York's principal entertainment district. There are now some 35 theatres in the vicinity of Times Square. The oldest is the Lyceum at 149 West 45th Street, which dates from 1903: all the earlier theatres have been pulled down.

Times Square itself (between 42nd and 47th Streets) has lost much of its former attraction: even the large illuminated signs are now outclassed by those of Las Vegas. Not much remains of the original architecture. Between 44th and 45th Streets stands a huge hotel with about 2000 rooms and an atrium. Although this building does not beautify Times Square it probably contributes to its rehabilitation. Nevertheless, Times Square is still one of New York's great tourist attractions, particularly in the evening. But if you go there late in the day you should keep your wallet in a safe place and beware of getting involved with dubious characters, for this area, on 42nd Street (between Seventh and Eighth Avenues) and 8th Avenue (between 42nd and 50th Streets), is probably the main stronghold of pornography, drug-taking and prostitution in

View of Times Square

Theatre tickets at half-price are obtainable here

New York. All attempts to clean up the area have failed, with the authorities scoring only minor and temporary successes in their campaign.

Tribeca   D/E10

Subway station
Canal Street (lines A, AA, E)

Tribeca – an acronym for "Triangle below Canal Street" – is the newest of New York's artists' quarters – rents in the adjoining district of SoHo (see entry) to the N having become too high for young artists trying to make a name for themselves.

Here, as in SoHo, whole floors of disused warehouses and factories have been converted into living accommodation; and here, too, numbers of restaurants, bars, discos and jazz and rock clubs have sprung up. There are also a number of galleries, mostly on upper floors.

The best known rock clubs are the Mudd Club (77 White Street, tel. 227 7777) and Tier 3 (225 West Broadway, tel. 226 9299). Interesting discos are TriBeCa (64 North Moore Street, tel. 925 8787) and Ones (111 Hudson Street, tel. 925 0011), which is mainly frequented by blacks.

Trinity Church   E11

Situation
Broadway and Wall Street

Subway stations
Wall Street (lines 4, 5),
Rector Street (lines 1, RR)

Buses
1, 6

Opening times
Mon.–Fri. 7 a.m.–6 p.m.,
Sat., Sun. and public
holidays 7 a.m.–4 p.m.

The first Trinity Church, built in 1698, was burned down in 1776. The second, built in 1788–90, was so dilapidated by 1839 that it was pulled down and replaced in 1846 by the present church, designed by the English architect Richard Upjohn. The bronze doors of the church, by Richard Morris Hunt, were a 20th c. addition, as were the Chapel of All Saints and the Bishop Manning Memorial Wing.

The Exhibit Room contains much interesting material on the early history of New York and of the church, which as the owner of valuable land in this area, is the wealthiest Episcopalian congregation in the city.

The church is surrounded on three sides by a churchyard dating from 1681, with the pyramid-shaped tomb of Alexander Hamilton, first Secretary of the US Treasury.

Also belonging to Trinity Church, which acquired most of its land under a grant from Queen Anne in 1705, is St Paul's Chapel (see entry).

Ukrainian Museum   F8

Address
203 Second Avenue

Subway station
Union Square
(lines 4, 5, 6, N, RR)

This museum, situated in an area still largely occupied by Ukranians, was founded in 1976. It is mainly devoted to Ukranian folk arts and crafts, including many examples of the famous *pysanky* (painted Easter eggs) as well as woven and embroidered textiles, pottery, wooden articles and metalwork. Most of the material dates from the 19th and 20th c.

The museum is open on Wednesdays, Saturdays and Sundays 1–5 p.m., Fridays 3–7 p.m.

*United Nations Headquarters

The United Nations Headquarters, built between 1946 and 1952 to the design of a team of internationally known architects, stands on a site previously occupied by slaughterhouses and light industry. The purchase of the site was made possible by the munificence of John D. Rockefeller Jr, and the building costs were met by an interest-free loan of 67 million dollars from the United States (since repaid).

At the S end of the complex is the Dag Hammarskjöld Library, built in 1961, a gift of the Ford Foundation. The other buildings are the General Assembly Building, the 39-storey glass and marble slab of the Secretariat Building and the rectangular Conference Building fronting on to East River.

The interior decoration and furnishings of the buildings were contributed by members of the United Nations.

When the General Assembly, the Security Council and other organs of the United Nations are in session the public are admitted within the limits of the seats available.

There are conducted tours of the UN buildings every 20 minutes or so throughout the day (9 a.m.–4.45 p.m.), for which a small charge is made.

Children under five are not admitted.

From Monday to Friday there are free film shows on the work of the United Nations, and on these days the delegates' dining room is open to the public at lunchtime (table reservations at the information desk in the main lobby).

Below the main lobby are:

The United Nations post office, at which the special UN stamps (valid only for letters and postcards posted here) can be bought.

A bookshop selling all UN publications.

Gift and souvenir shops selling articles from member nations.

UNICEF and UNESCO desks.

A coffee shop (open 9 a.m.–5 p.m.).

Situation
First Avenue and 47th Street

Subway station
Grand Central
(lines 4, 5, 6, 7, S)

Buses
15, 104, 106

Opening times
Daily 8 a.m.–5.30 p.m.

Conducted tours
9.15 a.m.–4.45 p.m.

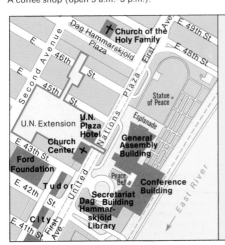

United Nations Headquarters

The **United Nations Organisation** (*UNO*), now generally known as the **United Nations** (*UN*), was constituted in 1945 at San Francisco, replacing the League of Nations (founded 1919). Its early meetings were held in London and at various temporary meeting-places in the New York area (Flushing, Lake Success); then in 1952 it moved into its present headquarters on East River. Its main elements are the General Assembly, the Security Council, the Economic and Social Council, the Trusteeship Council and the Secretariat.

United Nations Headquarters

In the neighbourhood

African-American Institute, 833 United Nations Plaza (corner of 46th Street): exhibitions of African art on the ground floor (tel. 949 5666).

Hammarskjöld Plaza, the eastward continuation of 47th Street beyond Second Avenue; there are temporary exhibitions of sculpture here.

Urban Center   E6

Situation Madison Avenue and
51st Street

Subway stations
51st Street (line 6),
Fifth Avenue (lines E, F)

Buses
1, 2, 3, 4

Opening times
Daily 11 a.m.–5 p.m.

Admission free

The Urban Center was formed at the end of 1980, when four organisations – the Municipal Art Society, the Architectural League, the New York branch of the American Institute of Artists and the Parks Council – took up their quarters at the N end of the famous row known as the Villard Houses, now incorporated in the new Palace Hotel. The main objective of these bodies is to promote the development of good architecture in an attractive environment, and they put on periodic ideas.

The Villard Houses, in an Italian Renaissance style modelled on the Palazzo della Cancelleria in Rome, were built by the New York architects McKim, Mead and White in 1884 for Henry Villard (originally named Heinrich Hilgard), publisher of the "New York Post", who emigrated from Bavaria to the United States in 1860 and within a very short time had achieved an established position and a fortune. The Villard Houses lie immediately behind St Patrick's Cathedral (see entry).

Van Cortlandt Mansion

This well-preserved stone-built house, erected in 1748 for a well-to-do New York family, stands in NW Bronx, at the S end of a park which now provides much-used facilities for a variety of ball games, but in the 18th c. was arable land.

The well-preserved furniture and furnishings date from the time when the house was built and from the latter part of the 18th c. Opening times are: Tuesday–Saturday 10 a.m.–4.45 p.m., Sunday 2–4.45 p.m.

Situation
Broadway, N of West 242nd Street (Bronx)

Subway station
242nd Street (line 1)

* Wall Street   E11

Wall Street has become a synonym for New York's Financial District, although this in fact extends in all directions from Wall Street.

The street takes its name from the wall built here to protect the Dutch settlement of New Amsterdam against British attack and Indian raids – a purpose which it failed to achieve. It is now a narrow canyon of a street into which the sun never penetrates, lined with banks, financial institutions and lawyers' offices; also two of the tallest skyscrapers in New York, which have no names other than their addresses of 40 and 60 Wall Street. On weekday afternoons Wall Street and the adjoining streets are so crowded with people that it is hardly possible to move; at weekends and on public holidays, however, the area is deserted.

At the corner of Wall Street and Broad Street are the fortress-like headquarters of the great banking house of J. P. Morgan, and diagonally opposite this is the New York Stock Exchange (see entry). A few yards N of Wall Street along Nassau Street is one of New York's most striking skyscrapers, the Chase Manhattan Bank (see Skyscrapers). Opposite the W end of Wall Street, on Broadway, stands Trinity Church (see entry). Up and down Broadway – N as far as Fulton Street, S to Bowling Green – are more of the skyscrapers, housing banks and offices, which give the district its characteristic aspect.

Subway stations
Wall Street (lines 4, 5), Rector Street (line RR)

Bus
6

* * Whitney Museum of American Art   E4

The Whitney Museum, the only museum in New York exclusively devoted to 20th c. American art, was founded in 1931 by Gertrude Vanderbilt Whitney, a wealthy sculptress and art patron. It was at first housed in a building in 8th Street (now occupied by an "alternative" art school); in 1954 it moved to premises in West 54th Street, behind the Museum of Modern Art (see entry); and when this building in turn became too small (and was taken over by the Museum of Modern Art) it was rehoused in its present Madison Avenue building, designed by the well-known architect Marcel Breuer. This is a five-storey inverted pyramid of grey granite and concrete, its severe exterior relieved by seven windows of varying size. The Museum now has 2750 sq. m (30,000 sq. ft) of display space, which can be subdivided according to requirements from time to time.

Situation
Madison Avenue and 75th Street

Subway station
77th Street (line 6)

Buses
1, 2, 3, 4

Opening times
Tues. 11 a.m.–8 p.m.,
Wed.–Sat. 11 a.m.–6 p.m.,
Sun. and public holidays
noon–6 p.m.

Whitney Museum of American Art

Whitney Museum of American Art

Admission free
Tues. after 5 p.m.

The Museum is entered by a concrete bridge, from which there is a view of the Sculpture Garden. On two of the four floors of display space there are regular special exhibitions, leaving far too little room for the steadily growing permanent collection. Every autumn there is an exhibition mainly devoted to items acquired during the preceding year. Leading American artists who are particularly well represented in the collection are the painters Stuart Davis, Jim Dine, Adolph Gottlieb, Jasper Johns and Mark Tobey and the sculptors Alexander Calder, Louise Nevelson and William Zorach.

The Museum also possesses a collection of some 2000 paintings, drawings and prints bequeathed to it by Edward Hopper.

There are daily showings of experimental films in the Museum: for details of the programme telephone 288 9601.

The Whitney Museum also has a downtown branch, which has been housed since the end of 1980 in a former police headquarters at 40 Old Slip, near East River (tel. 483 0011). This branch organises architectural walks in southern Manhattan (Tuesdays and Thursdays at 12.30 p.m.) and also puts on concerts and other shows on Wednesdays at 12.30 p.m. (admission free).

In the newly erected building of the Philip Morris Co. at the corner of Park Avenue and 42nd Street, another branch museum was opened in 1983. Temporary exhibitions from the museum are open from Monday to Friday from 11 a.m.–6 p.m. and on Thursdays until 7.30 p.m. Admission is free. Tel. 878 2550.

Manhattan Bridge and downtown skyline

World Trade Center D/E11

The tallest building in New York, this is also the most controversial, for although its imposing dimensions and monumental quality cannot be denied, it has come under heavy fire for damaging the townscape of Manhattan. The twin towers (420 m (1380 ft) high, 110 floors), designed by Minoru Yamasaki and built between 1970 and 1977, are criticised as architecturally uninteresting – though they have had considerable influence on New York architecture. The Observation Deck on the 107th floor of the N tower offers powerful competition to the observatory of the Empire State Building (see entry), although the views from these two outlook points are very different (information: tel. 466 7377). On the same floor of the other tower is New York's highest restaurant, Windows on the World, which operates as a club but is open to the public at lunch and dinner time. Here you can have dinner and a breathtaking view at the same time, provided that you get a table near the window (reservation essential: tel. 938 1111). Men must wear a collar and tie and a jacket.

Also in the World Trade Center complex are the US Customhouse and the new Vista Hotel.

At the foot of the twin towers is a plaza larger than St Mark's Square in Venice – a comparison which was actually drawn by a New York real estate man – but appears, unlike St Mark's Square, to serve no particular function. In the plaza is a pool with a slowly revolving bronze globe by the German sculptor Fritz Koenig.

Situation
Between Church, Vesey, Dey and Liberty Streets

Subway stations
Cortlandt Street
(lines 1, RR),
Chambers Street (line AA)

Bus
10

Opening times
Observation Deck:
9.30 a.m.–9.30 p.m.

111

Practical Information

Airlines

Air Canada
488 Madison Avenue, tel. 421 8000

Air France
666 Fifth Avenue, tel. 841 7300

Alitalia
666 Fifth Avenue, tel. 262 4422

Austrian Airlines
608 Fifth Avenue, 507, tel. 265 6350

British Airways
530 Fifth Avenue, tel. 687 1600

KLM
437 Madison Avenue, tel. 759 3600

Lufthansa
680 Fifth Avenue, tel. 397 9250

PanAm
200 Park Avenue, tel. 973 4000

Swissair
608 Fifth Avenue, tel. 995 8400

TWA
Nine branches in Manhattan: tel. 290 2121

Airports

J. F. Kennedy International Airport

This, the largest of New York's three commercial airports, lies on Jamaica Bay, 16 miles from the city centre. Passengers arrive in the International Arrival Building, except those flying with PanAm, TWA or British Airways, which all have their own terminals.

Getting to and from Manhattan

By taxi
The fare at present ranges between $22 and $26 according to the traffic, plus $1.25 for the tunnel or bridge toll and a $4 tip.

By Carey Bus
To East Side Terminal, First Avenue and 38th Street (from which a taxi will probably be necessary to complete the journey) and the Hilton Hotel.
Fare at present $6. The buses run every 20 minutes 6 a.m.– 11 p.m., at longer intervals thereafter.

By JFK Express
Four bus/subway stops in Manhattan, Avenue of the Americas
(at 4th, 34th, 42nd and 57th Streets).
Fare at present $5. Buses every 20 minutes. (Not recommended
if you have a lot of luggage.)

By service bus
Take the Q10 bus to its terminus at Kew Gardens; then subway
line E or F to Manhattan.
Fare $1.50. The cheapest way, but the slowest, and only
possible if you have not much luggage.

By helicopter
To East 34th Street (East River).
Fare at present $37.14 (plus tax). Flights every hour. Check-in
time ten minutes prior to departure. Quickest way (18 minutes).

There are also connections with places outside New York
including New Jersey, Westchester, Long Island, etc.
Information about departure times can be obtained from the
transport companies (toll-free telephones in the arrival halls).
Taxi journeys to places outside New York cost twice the fare
shown on the meter, plus bridge or tunnel tolls.

*Connections with places
outside New York*

Carey Line buses run to La Guardia Airport hourly 7.30 a.m.–
1.30 p.m. and half-hourly 1.30–9.20 p.m.
Salem Transportation Inc. have cars running to Newark Airport
9 a.m.–9 p.m.
Helicopter flights operate between all the airports 6 a.m.–
9.30 p.m.

*Connections with other New
York airports*

La Guardia Airport, also in Queens, is only eight miles from the
city centre.

*La Guardia International
Airport*

By taxi
Fare about $12 plus $1.25 bridge or tunnel toll and $1.50–$2 tip.

*Getting to and from
Manhattan*

150th Street Entrance

Medical Building
Post Office
Animal Shelter
American
Olympic
N.Y. Helicopters
United
Finnair
Eastern
Police &
General
Aviation
Building
Northwest
Delta
Pan American
Aeroflot
Alia (Jordan)
Avianca (Columbia)
P = Parking
Control
Tower
WEST WING
DEPARTURE
AREA
International
Arrivals Building
EAST WING
DEPARTURE
AREA
TWA
USA
TWA
Overseas

British Airways
Air Canada
Air Jamaica
Capitol
South African
TAP (Portugal)

Czechoslovak Syrian Arab
Iran Air   Tarom (Romania)
Lot (Poland)   U.S. Air
Sata (Azores) Yugoslav

John F. Kennedy International Airport

WEST WING
DEPARTURE AREA
Air France
Air India
Air Afrique
Air Panamá
Alitalia
Balair (Switzerland)
El Al (Israel)
Sabena (Belgium)
SAS (Scandinavia)
Swissair
Transamerica

EAST WING
DEPARTURE AREA
Aer Lingus (Ireland)
Aerolinias Aregentinas

Aeroméxico
Condor
Dominicana
Iberia (Spain)
Icelandair
(Flugleidir)
JAL (Japan)
KLM (Netherlands)
ALM (Netherlands
Antilles)
Lan-Chile
Lufthansa
Maersk (Denmark)
PIA (Pakistan)
Royal Air Maroc
Varig (Brazil)
Viasa (Venezuela)
World (California)

Practical Information

By Carey Bus
Fare to East Side Terminal $5. Buses every 15 minutes
6.45 a.m.–11.15 p.m.

By service bus
Q33 bus to 74th Street/Roosevelt Avenue subway station,
connecting with lines E, F, GG, N and 7. Fare $1.50. Not
recommended if you have heavy luggage.

By helicopter
From American Airlines Gate 9. Fare at present $26.67 (plus
tax). Check-in time ten minutes prior to departure. Quickest
way (18 minutes).

Newark International Airport

On Newark Bay (New Jersey), 15 miles from the city centre,
but a quicker journey than to or from the other airports, since
the traffic on the road is not so heavy.

Getting to and from New
York

By taxi
Taxis are expensive, since the fare is double the amount shown
on the meter, plus tunnel toll and tip.

By Carey Bus
To World Trade Center (Mon.–Sat. only). Fare $5.

By Transport of New Jersey buses
To bus station at Eighth Avenue and 40th Street. Fare $4.50.
Buses every 15–30 minutes, 5.30 a.m. to 45 minutes after
midnight.

By helicopter

There are helicopter connections between all the commercial
airports and with Manhattan.

Antiques

New York has so many antique dealers (11 pages of them in the
"Yellow Pages" telephone directory) and they are so highly
specialised in particular fields that the best way of finding what
you want is to consult the classified "Antique Dealers' Guide"
in the Yellow Pages.

Auction rooms

Almost every day there are auctions of works of art, carpets,
jewellery and miscellaneous objets d'art in New York. The
major auctions, which are also great social occasions, are
usually held in the evening at Sotheby Parke Bernet and
Christie's.
There is always provision for viewing the objects to be sold
before the auction.

Christie's, 502 Park Avenue (59th Street), tel. 546 1000
Christie's East, 219 East 67th Street, tel. 570 4141
Open Mon.–Sat. 10 a.m.–5 p.m.

William Doyle Galleries, 175 East 87th Street, tel. 427 2730
Open: irregularly

Phillips, 572 East 72nd Street, tel. 570 4842; 867 Madison
Avenue (72nd Street), tel. 472 1000
Open Mon.–Sat. noon–5 p.m.

Sotheby Parke Bernet, Inc., 1334 York Avenue, corner of 72nd
Street, tel. 472 3400
Open Tues.–Sat. 9.30 a.m.–5 p.m., Sun. 1–5 p.m.

Banks

Most banks are open Mon.–Fri. 9 a.m.–3 p.m. Some are also
open on Saturday mornings.

Banking hours

Exchange offices are usually open 9 a.m.–6 p.m.
In the International Arrival Building of J. F. Kennedy Airport:
Exchange office of Citybank and Perera Co. (open until
midnight, except Sun.).
In New York City:
American Express, 374 Park Avenue
Thomas Cook Travel, 18 East 48th Street
Perera Co., 630 Fifth Avenue and 41 East 42nd Street
Harald Reuter and Co., PanAm Building, 200 Park Avenue
Foreign currency can also be changed in various foreign banks
on Fifth Avenue, as indicated by signs in the window.

Exchange offices
(Bureaux de change)

Since there may be difficulty about changing foreign money in
the United States (no provision for changing money in hotels,
time-consuming checks by banks) and since you are likely to
lose on the exchange, the best plan is to take US dollars with
you – a limited amount in cash but most of your money in the
form of dollar travellers' cheques, obtained either from your
own bank or from a branch of American Express. Eurocheques
and cheque cards are of no use.
If your American Express cheques are lost or stolen you can
usually have them replaced by the nearest American Express
branch on presentation of the sales advice issued when you
bought the cheques.
Visa cheques are also widely used now.

Travellers' cheques

Bathing beaches

Since the New York boroughs of Brooklyn and Queens are
situated by the sea, they have bathing beaches which are
readily accessible free of charge but tend to be very
overcrowded during the season.
The Atlantic is slow to warm up, and the water is therefore rarely
warm enough for bathing before the end of June. The season
lasts only until the beginning of September, though bathing is
usually possible until the end of that month.

Coney Island and Brighton Beach
Subway: line N, D or F to Stillwell Avenue or Brighton Beach;
line A to Rockaway and Far Rockaway.

Within the city

Beach on Long Island

Outside the city

Jones Beach State Park
Long Island Railroad from Pennsylvania Station to Freeport, then bus connecting with train. Information about departures: tel. 739 4200.
Perhaps the most beautiful beach on the E coast of the United States (12 miles of sand, fresh-water and sea-water pools, restaurants, open-air theatre).

Fire Island
Long Island Railroad to Sayville, Bayshore and Patchogue, where there are also mainland ferryboat lines.
Thirty-two miles of Nautical Seashore. Fishing, swimming and walking in natural unspoilt landscape, as well as numerous facilities.

Boat excursions

The only day trip, run by the Hudson River Day Line, is up the Hudson River to Bear Mountain and West Point, site of the United States Military Academy. From here it is possible to visit Hyde Park, former home of President F. D. Roosevelt, where his papers are preserved in a specially built library.
Departures from the end of May to mid September, daily at 10 a.m., from Pier 81 (end of 41st Street), returning at 7 p.m. No departures on Mondays and Fridays in June.
Information: tel. 279 5151.

Bookshops

Barnes and Noble, 105 Fifth Avenue (18th Street), tel. 807 0099 (New York's best university bookshop)
B. Dalton, 666 Fifth Avenue (52nd Street), tel. 247 1740
Doubleday, 724 Fifth Avenue (57th Street), tel. 397 0550
Doubleday, 673 Fifth Avenue (53rd Street), tel. 953 4805
Gotham Book Mart, 41 West 47th Street, tel. 719 4448
Rizzoli, 712 Fifth Avenue (56th Street), tel. 397 3700
Scribner's, 597 Fifth Avenue (48th Street), tel. 486 4070

General bookshops

Cinemabilia
10 West 13th Street, tel. 989 8519
Film

Special interests

Hacker Art Books
54 West 57th Street, tel. 757 1450
Art

Jaap Rietman
167 Spring Street (SoHo), tel. 966 7044
Art

Wittenborn Art Books
1018 Madison Avenue, tel. 288 1558
Art

New York Bound Bookshop
43 West 54th Street, tel. 245 8503
New York City

Samuel Weiser
740 Broadway (8th Street), tel. 777 6363
Metaphysics

Drama Bookshop
723 Seventh Avenue, tel. 944 0505
The theatre

Argosy, 116 East 59th Street, tel. 753 4455
Barnes and Noble, 128 Fifth Avenue (18th Street), tel. 807 0099
Barnes and Noble, 600 Fifth Avenue (47th Street), tel. 765 0590
Strand's, 828 Broadway (12th Street), tel. 473 1452

Secondhand and antiquarian

See Business hours

Shop hours

Breakdown assistance

If you have a breakdown in a hired car the car hire firm should be informed in the first place (see Car hire).
Otherwise the "Yellow Pages" of the New York telephone directory give a full list of repair garages.
Visitors bringing in their own car which is not a US make should ensure that it is in perfect mechanical order, since spare parts

not in accordance with American standards may be difficult to obtain – though in the larger towns there is usually a firm which sells or repairs foreign cars.

Business hours

Shops	There are no regulations limiting shop hours, and shops and restaurants in New York can stay open as long as the owner likes: some shops, indeed – including supermarkets – are open seven days a week and 24 hours a day. The large department stores tend to be open 9.45 a.m.– 6.45 p.m., on Mondays and Thursdays (and during the pre-Christmas period every evening) until 9 p.m., on Sundays from 11 a.m. or noon to 5 p.m. Many small shops keep similar hours, particularly in areas where there are department stores.
Public transport	All forms of public transport operate round the clock.
Bars	Since there are no statutory hours, bars as well as restaurants can stay open as long as they like.
Chemists (drugstores)	Mon.–Sat. 9 a.m.–6 p.m.
Banks	Mon.–Fri. 9 a.m.–3 p.m.
Museums	See the entries for particular museums and the list of museums on p. 139.
Post offices	Usually Mon.–Fri. 8.30 a.m.–6 p.m., Sat. 9 a.m.–noon.

Car hire

There is little point in driving your own car or a hired car in New York City, with its heavy traffic and inadequate parking facilities, and the best way of getting about is by public transport or by taxi; but if you want to see something of the surrounding area or to continue your journey to some other part of the United States a car is essential.

To hire a car it is necessary to produce a valid driving licence: British licences and those of certain other countries are acceptable. It is useful also to have a credit card (American Express, Mastercharge or Visa), since otherwise it may be necessary to put down a considerable sum as surety.

There are numerous car hire firms in New York, some internationally known, others local; some of them also hire out cars with drivers. They are listed in the "Yellow Pages" telephone directory under the heading "Automobile renting and leasing".

You can arrange for a hire by telephone, by ringing one of the large car rental firms at the following numbers:
Avis: (1–800) 331 1212
Budget Rent-a-Car: 541 4222
Dollar Rent-a-Car: 567 0600
Hertz: (1–800) 654 3131
National Car: (1–800) 328 4567
Olins Rent-a-Car: 581 6161

Chemists

See Drugstores

Churches and synagogues

Over a hundred different religious denominations are represented in New York. Some hotels have lists giving the times of services (usually at 11 a.m. on Sunday).

See A to Z	Cathedral Church of St John the Divine

Lexington Avenue and 55th Street — Central Synagogue
Subway: Lexington Avenue (lines E and F)
New York's oldest synagogue, a Moorish-style building designed by Henry Fernbach (1872). The interior is more attractive than the exterior, apart from the two domes topped by stars.

Broadway and 10th Street — Grace Episcopal Church
Subway: Astor Place (line 6), 8th Street (line RR)
A neo-Gothic building erected by James Renwick, an engineer and amateur architect, in 1846. One of New York's more beautiful churches, it has considerable grace and sensitivity.

Washington Square South — Judson Memorial Church
Subway: 8th Street (line RR), 4th Street (lines A, AA, CC, D, E, F)
Built in 1892 by McKim, Mead and White: in an eclectic Romanesque style with Italian Renaissance features, it dominated the square for many years before being dwarfed by surrounding buildings. The marble Washington Arch in the square was built by the same architects in the same year.

See A to Z — St Bartholomew's Protestant Episcopal Church

See A to Z — St Mark's in the Bowery

See A to Z — St Patrick's Cathedral

See A to Z — St Paul's Chapel

Lexington Avenue and 54th Street — St Peter's Church
Subway: Lexington Avenue (lines E and F), 51st Street (line 6)
One of New York's few modern churches, built by Hugh Stubbins in 1977 together with the Citicorp skyscraper. It occupies the same site as its neo-Gothic predecessor, which sold its rights to the air space above the site to Citicorp. The church, surmounted by a vaulted granite roof, has something of a sculptured effect. A notable feature of the interior is the Erol Baker Chapel, decorated by the sculptress Louise Nevelson.

Fifth Avenue and 53rd Street — St Thomas's Church
Subway: Fifth Avenue (lines E and F)
A Gothic church built by Bertram Goodhue in 1914, showing

Temple Emanu-El, the synagogue of New York's wealthiest Jewish community

a mingling of English and French stylistic elements; an asymmetric building, designed to fit into a street intersection, which asserts its position alongside the neighbouring skyscrapers.

Temple Emanu-El

Fifth Avenue and 65th Street
Buses: 1, 2, 3, 4
A synagogue belonging to the wealthiest Jewish community in New York, built by Robert D. Kohn, Charles Butler and Clarence Stein in 1929. It is one of the city's largest places of worship (larger than St Patrick's Cathedral), with seating for 2500. Notable features are the neo-Romanesque arch over the entrance and the Byzantine-influenced interior.

Trinity Church

See A to Z

Church music

See Music

Cinemas

New York's cinemas are too numerous to count. Its 50 first-run cinemas are concentrated in the area of Times Square, on 57th Street and on Third and Second Avenues between 57th and 72nd Streets, so that visitors to New York are likely to come across a good many of them in the course of their sightseeing. Programmes are listed in the newspapers.

The following cinemas show only older films:
Bleecker Street Cinema, 144 Bleecker Street, tel. 674 2560
Cinema Village, 22 East 12th Street, tel. 924 3363
St Mark's Cinema, 133 Second Avenue (8th Street), tel. 533 9292
Theatre 80 St Mark's, 80 St Mark's Place, tel. 254 7400
Carnegie Hall Cinema, Seventh Avenue and 57th Street, tel. 757 2131
New Yorker I and II, 2904 Broadway (88th Street), tel. 874 9189
Regency, 1987 Broadway (67th Street), tel. 724 3700

Older films

The cinema in the Museum of Modern Art, 11 West 53rd Street, shows foreign films old and new, usually as part of a series, with a programme which changes daily.

Foreign films

Mainly showings of avant-garde films:
Anthology Archives, 80 Wooster Street, tel. 226 0010
Film Forum, 57 Watts Street, tel. 431 1590
Millennium Film Workshop, 66 East 4th Street, tel. 673 0090
Public Theatre, 425 Lafayette Avenue, tel. 598 7100

Experimental films

Held annually from end September to mid October in the Alice Tully Hall (see A to Z, Lincoln Center): a programme of some 20 films new to New York, mostly from Europe. No prizes are awarded.

New York Film Festival

Climate

New York City lies in roughly the same latitude as Naples in Italy, but in summer (June to mid September) New York is hotter and in winter (December to March) considerably colder – mainly as a result of the wind – than Naples. In general it has long periods of clear weather (250–300 days), since depressions usually pass over quickly and anticyclones remain constant. The best times to visit New York are in May and from mid September to the beginning of December. The height of summer should be avoided if possible: in air-conditioned buildings it is tolerable, but the high humidity of the air makes it oppressively close in the streets. In summer hotel rooms tend to be rather too cool, while in winter they are usually overheated.

Snow rarely falls before January. The highest summer temperature ever recorded in New York was 41 °C (106 °F), the lowest winter temperature −24 °C (−11 °F); but such extreme temperatures seldom occur.

°F	°C
0	−18
10	−12
20	−5
32	0
50	10
68	20
86	30
95	35
212	100

Conversion factors:

°F to °C: $(°F - 32) \times \frac{5}{9}$

°C to °F: $°C \times \frac{9}{5} + 32$

Relationship °F/°C:

°F:°C = 9:5

°C:°F = 5:9

Conversion table (F/C)

Practical Information

Weather information

Weather forecasts are included in almost all the news bulletins given at regular intervals on radio and television.

Consulates

United Kingdom: 845 Third Avenue, tel. 752 8400
Canada: 1251 Avenue of the Americas, tel. 586 2400

Credit cards

It is advisable to have one or more of the major credit cards (American Express, Mastercharge, Visa, Diner's Club, Carte Blanche), which are often regarded as a better indication of creditworthiness than the possession of cash. They can be used for the payment of bills of all kinds (in hotels, restaurants and shops), for the purchase of air tickets, in place of a deposit when hiring a car or as evidence of identity.

Currency

The US unit of currency is the dollar ($), which consists of 100 cents. There are notes (bills) for 1, 2, 5, 10, 20, 50 and 100 dollars and coins in denominations of 1 cent (a penny), 5 cents (a nickel), 10 cents (a dime), 25 cents (a quarter) and – less commonly found – 50 cents (a half-dollar) and a dollar.
The exchange rate of the dollar against sterling (and other currencies) fluctuates considerably.

Since it is not so easy to change money in New York (or elsewhere in the United States) as in Europe, it is a good idea to get some dollar bills and small change before arriving in New York.

Import and export of currency

There are no restrictions on the import or export of either American or foreign currency; but if you are taking in more than 5000 dollars a customs declaration must be filled in on the aircraft.

Travellers' cheques

See Banks

Customs regulations

Visitors to the United States may take in, duty-free, personal effects including clothing, articles of personal adornment, toilet articles and hunting, fishing and photographic equipment; one litre of alcoholic beverages (wine, beer, spirits) if over 21; 200 cigarettes or 50 cigars or 3 lb of tobacco, or proportionate amounts of each; and gifts up to a total value of 100 dollars. Items which cannot be taken into the United States include meat, fruit, vegetables and ornamental plants.

Department stores

Alexander's
Lexington Avenue and 58th Street
Open Mon.–Sat. 10 a.m.–9 p.m., Sun. noon–5 p.m.

Alexander's
World Trade Center
Open Mon.–Sat. 8.30 a.m.–6 p.m.

B. Altman
Fifth Avenue and 34th Street
Open Mon.–Wed. and Fri.–Sat. 10 a.m.–6 p.m., Thurs.
10 a.m.–8 p.m.; closed Sun.

Bloomingdale's
Lexington Avenue and 59th Street
Open Mon. and Thurs. 9.45 a.m.–9 p.m., Tues., Wed., Fri. and
Sat. 9.45 a.m.–6 p.m.; closed Sun.

Gimbel's
Broadway and 33rd Street
Open Thurs. and Fri. 10 a.m.–8.30 p.m., Mon., Wed. and Sat.
10 a.m.–6 p.m., Sun. 11 a.m.–6 p.m.

Gimbel's East
Lexington Avenue and 86th Street
Open: as for Gimbel's

Macy's: New York's largest department store

Lord and Taylor
Fifth Avenue and 38th Street
Open Thurs. 10 a.m.–8 p.m., Mon., Wed., Fri. and Sat.
10 a.m.–6 p.m.; closed Sun.

Macy's
Broadway and 34th Street
Open Mon., Thurs. and Fri. 9.45 a.m.–8.30 p.m., Tues. and
Wed. 9.45 a.m.–6.45 p.m., Sat. 9.45 a.m,–6 p.m., Sun. noon–
5 p.m.

Ohrbach's
5 East 34th Street
Open Mon.–Wed. and Fri. 10 a.m.–6.45 p.m., Thurs.
10 a.m.–8.30 p.m., Sat. 10 a.m.–6 p.m., Sun. noon–5 p.m.

Saks Fifth Avenue
Fifth Avenue and 50th Street
Open Thurs. 10 a.m.–8.30 p.m., Mon.–Wed., Fri. and Sat.
10 a.m.–6 p.m.; closed Sun.

Doctors

See Emergency calls

Drugstores

The American drugstore is a very different kind of place from a
European chemist's shop or pharmacy. In most drugstores the
supply of medicines on prescription is only a small part of their
business, and many of them are more like small department
stores offering a wide range of wares, including facilities for
eating and drinking.

Information   For a list of drugstores in New York consult the "Yellow Pages"
telephone directory.

Opening times   Usually 9 a.m.–6 p.m. Some stay open until 9 p.m. or even
midnight.

All-night pharmacy   The following Manhattan pharmacy is open 24 hours a day:
Kaufman Pharmacy, 50th Street and Lexington Avenue, tel.
755 2266.

Emergency service   There is no organised night emergency service. In case of
emergency it is always possible to go to the nearest hospital
(see Hospitals), since all hospitals have pharmacies. Alterna-
tively telephone 265 3546 or 755 2266.

Electricity

110–115 volt, 60 cycle AC. If you have an electric razor, hair-
drier or iron you should take an adapter with you. If you forget
or lose your adapter you can get one in a hardware store or a
department store. (The hotel porter will be able to tell you
where to go.)

Emergency calls

Dial 911   Police, fire, ambulance
In Manhattan telephone 879 1000.   To call a doctor

Events

Chinese New Year celebrations in Chinatown. The time,   January
determined by the Chinese lunar calendar, ranges between the
end of January and mid February.
Information: tel. 687 1300.
Mid January: National Boat Show in the New York Coliseum
on Columbus Circle/West 59th Street (tel. 757 5000).
End of January: Greater New York Auto Show in the New York
Coliseum, Columbus Circle/West 59th Street.
End of January: Winter Antiques Show in 7th Regiment
Armory, Park Avenue and East 68th Street (tel. 288 0200).

Mid February: National Antiques Show in Madison Square   February
Garden, 4 Penn Plaza (tel. 564 4400). New York's largest
antiques show, lasting a week.
Mid February: Westminster Kennel Club Dog Show in Madison
Square Garden, 4 Penn Plaza (tel. 564 4400). A two-day show
of all breeds.

17 March: St Patrick's Day, with New York's largest and most   March
spectacular parade by Irish Americans along Broadway from
44th to 86th Street, starting at 11 a.m. Many decorated floats
and bands.
Ringling Brothers and Barnum and Bailey Circus in Madison
Square Garden, 4 Penn Plaza (tel. 564 4400). This three-ring
circus, continuing into June, puts on its show in New York's
largest auditorium.

Easter Day: Easter Parade on Fifth Avenue (49th to 59th   March or April
Street), noon–2.30 p.m.

From April to mid May there is a magnificent display of spring   April
flowers in the Rockefeller Center on Fifth Avenue.

13 May: Parade on Fifth Avenue commemorating the murdered   May
black leader and Nobel prizewinner Martin Luther King on his
birthday (information: tel. 687 1300).
Ninth Avenue International Festival, held on Ninth Avenue,
between 37th and 59th Streets, on a weekend in May
(information: tel. 687 1300). An occasion displaying all the
ethnic variety of Ninth Avenue, with its numerous shops and
stalls.
Washington Square Outdoor Art Show. On three weekends
during May painters, sculptors and other artists and craftsmen
offer their work for sale around Washington Square, particularly in University Place, Fifth Avenue and the adjoining side
streets (information: tel. 982 6255).

Jazz Festival, lasting three weeks, with performances in many   June
concert halls (information: tel. 787 2020) and on the streets
(tel. 873 0733).

New Year celebrations in Chinatown

Good Friday procession in Lower East Side

End of June until August: performances of plays by Shakespeare and other authors in the Delacorte Theater in Central Park; no charge for admission (information: tel. 535 5630 or 598 7100).

4 July: Independence Day, with celebrations in Battery Park, noon–7 p.m. (information: tel. 687 1300), a nautical event on the Hudson (information: tel. 687 1300), and a firework display on the Hudson at 9.15 p.m., seen at its best from Riverside Park between 80th and 105th Streets (information: tel. 695 4400).

July

Mid August: "Lincoln Center Out-of-Doors", a street festival on the Lincoln Center Plaza (Broadway and 65th Street), with a programme of events, 11 a.m.–8 p.m. daily (information: tel. 877 1800).

August

First Sunday: West Indian American Day Carnival on Eastern Parkway and Utica Avenue in Brooklyn, with an exotic parade (information: tel. 772 5709).
Third Saturday: Steuban Parade by German Americans on Fifth Avenue (from 44th to 86th Street).
Mid September: Feast of San Gennaro (St Januarius) in Little Italy (Mulberry Street, Lower Manhattan), a colourful fiesta with many stalls, sideshows, etc. (information: tel. 226 9546). Washington Square Outdoor Art Show, on three weekends. See above under May.

September

Columbus Day Parade of Italian Americans on Fifth Avenue (varying dates).
19 October: Pulaski Day Parade by Poles (information: tel. 687 1300).
End of October: International Horse Show in Madison Square Garden, 4 Penn Plaza (information: tel. 562 8000).
Last Sunday: New York City Marathon, run on a 26-mile course through the five boroughs, starting from the Staten Island side of the Verrazano Narrows Bridge and ending at the Tavern-on-the-Green in Central Park. Some 10,000 runners take part. Information: tel. 595 4141.

October

Fourth Thursday: Thanksgiving Day. A Thanksgiving Parade is organised by Macy's, the great department store, mainly intended for children; it starts from Central Park (West 77th Street) at 9.15 a.m., heads S to Columbus Circle and then along Broadway to end at 34th Street in front of the store. Information: tel. 687 1300.

November

Beginning of December: A huge Christmas tree is erected in the Rockefeller Center, Where there is carol singing and other events (information: tel. 489 4300).
31 December: Tens of thousands of New Yorkers gather in Times Square to see the New Year in. During the last minute of the old year a large ball illuminated by nearly 200 bulbs descends a flagpole on top of the 1 Times Square Building.

December

To find out what is going on in New York consult the newspapers ("Daily News", "New York Times,", "New York Post"); the following publications are also useful:
"Village Voice" and "SoHo Weekly News" (both weekly) give

What's on?

127

the complete programmes of the small "off-Broadway" theatres.

The "Big Apple Guide" is published annually by the New York Convention and Visitors Bureau (see Tourist information).

"Village Voice", which is published each Wednesday, prints more or less completely the programmes of the off-off-Broadway theatres.

Ferries

Manhattan to Staten Island	Staten Island Ferry

Departures from Battery Park every 20 minutes Mon.–Fri., every 30 minutes Sat. and Sun., every 45–60 minutes between midnight and 5 a.m.

Information: 248 8097.

The crossing takes about half an hour each way. The return fare is 25 cents, making this one of the cheapest as well as most rewarding trips in New York, offering – particularly on the return journey – a magnificent view of the skyscrapers of lower Manhattan.

Manhattan to Ellis Island	See A to Z, Ellis Island

Food

Even if you lack time, money or appetite for a meal in one of New York's countless restaurants (see entry) you need never go hungry, since there are plenty of opportunities all over the city for picking up a hamburger, a hot dog or one of the other popular forms of "fast food".

Hamburgers

A hamburger is a sandwich consisting of a patty of ground or chopped meat, seasoned with onions, cheese, etc., between two halves of a roll. The price ranges between 75 cents and $2.

Hot dogs

A hot dog is a frankfurter, with mustard and sauerkraut, served in a split roll. Price about 80 cents.

Pizzas

A pizza consists of a flat dough base spread with tomato sauce, pieces of sausage, cheese and seasoning, and is eaten hot.

Sandwiches

The most popular American form of sandwich is made of rye bread and corned beef, roast beef or pastrami (a highly seasoned cut of smoked beef), with a slice of gherkin.

Brunch

A New York speciality is brunch, a cross between breakfast and lunch which is served in most hotels and restaurants on Saturdays and Sundays from about 11 a.m. to the early afternoon. The cost ranges between $5 and $15.

Galleries

New York has over 400 art galleries, mostly concentrated in two areas of the city, between 57th and 86th Streets (particularly in 57th Street and Madison Avenue) and in SoHo (on West Broadway and adjoining streets). The following are some of the principal galleries, listed in alphabetical order. Some of them specialise in particular genres or periods.

Aberbach Fine Art, 988 Madison Avenue, tel. 988 1100 Uptown galleries
A.C.A. Galleries, 21 East 67th Street, tel. 628 2440
Babcock Galleries, 20 East 67th Street, tel. 535 9355
Bodley, 1063 Madison Avenue, tel. 249 2155
Grace Borgenicht, 725 Fifth Avenue, tel. 247 2111
Carus Gallery, 872 Madison Avenue, tel. 879 4660
Cordier and Ekstrom, 417 East 75th Street, tel. 988 8857
Sid Deutsch, 20 West 57th Street, tel. 765 4722
Terry Dintenfass, 50 West 57th Street, tel. 581 2268
Robert Elkon Gallery, 1063 Madison Avenue, tel. 535 3940
André Emmerich Gallery, 41 East 57th Street, tel. 752 0124
Ronald Feldman Fine Arts, 33 East 74th Street, tel. 249 4050
David Findlay Galleries, 964 Madison Avenue, tel. 249 2909
Wally Findlay, 17 East 57th Street, tel. 421 5390
Fischbach, 29 West 57th Street, tel. 759 2345
Forum Gallery, 1018 Madison Avenue, tel. 772 7666
Allan Frumkin Gallery, 50 West 57th Street, tel. 757 6655
Gimpel and Weitzenhoffer, 1040 Madison Avenue,
tel. 628 1897
James Goodman Gallery, 1020 Madison Avenue, tel. 427 8383
Graham Gallery, 1014 Madison Avenue, tel. 535 5767
Gruenebaum Gallery, 38 East 57th Street, tel. 838 8245
Hamilton Gallery, 20 West 57th Street, tel. 765 5915
Hirschl and Adler Galleries, 21 East 70th Street, tel. 535 8810
Leonard Hutton Galleries, 33 East 74th Street, tel. 249 9700
Martha Jackson Gallery, 521 West 57th Street, tel. 586 4200
Sidney Janis Gallery, 110 West 57th Street, tel. 586 0110
Kennedy Galleries, 40 West 57th Street, tel. 541 9600
Coe Kerr Gallery, 49 East 82nd Street, tel. 628 1340
Knoedler and Co., 19 East 70th Street, tel. 794 0550
Kraushaar Galleries, 724 Fifth Avenue, tel. 307 5730
La Boëtie, 9 East 82nd Street, tel. 535 4865
Lefebre Gallery, 47 East 77th Street, tel. 744 3384
Pierre Matisse Gallery, 41 East 57th Street, tel. 355 6269
Tibor de Nagy Gallery, 29 West 57th Street, tel. 421 3780
Newhouse Galleries, 19 East 66th Street, tel. 879 2700
Pace Gallery of New York, 32 East 57th Street, tel. 421 3292
Betty Parsons Gallery, 24 West 57th Street, tel. 247 7480
Perls Galleries, 1016 Madison Avenue, tel. 472 3200
Serge Sabarsky Gallery, 987 Madison Avenue, tel. 628 6281
A. M. Sachs Gallery, 29 West 57th Street, tel. 421 8686
Saidenberg Gallery, 1018 Madison Avenue, tel. 288 3387
Spencer A. Samuels and Co., 13 East 76th Street, tel. 988 4556
Schaeffer Galleries, 983 Park Avenue, tel. 535 6410
Robert Schoellkopf Gallery, 825 Madison Avenue,
tel. 879 4638
Solomon and Co. Fine Art, 959 Madison Avenue, tel. 737 8200
Ira Spanierman, 50 East 78th Street, tel. 879 7085
Staempfli Gallery, 47 East 77th Street, tel. 535 1919
Touchstone Gallery, 29 West 57th Street, tel. 826 6111
Vasarely Center, 1015 Madison Avenue, tel. 744 2332
Weintraub Gallery, 992 Madison Avenue, tel. 879 1195
Wildenstein and Co., 19 East 64th Street, tel. 879 0500
Daniel Wolf, 30 West 57th Street, tel. 586 8432

Practical Information

Zabriskie Gallery, 521 West 57th Street, tel. 832 9034
Andre Zarre, 41 East 57th Street, tel. 752 0498

SoHo galleries

Mary Boone Galleries, 417 West Broadway, tel. 431 1818, and
420 West Broadway, tel. 966 2114
Susan Caldwell, 383 West Broadway, tel. 966 6500
Leo Castelli Gallery, 420 West Broadway, tel. 431 5160
Paula Cooper Gallery, 155 Wooster Street, tel. 677 4390
O.K. Harris, 383 West Broadway, tel. 431 3600
Nancy Hoffman, 429 West Broadway, tel. 966 6676
Max Hutchinson Gallery, 138 Greene Street, tel. 966 3066
Louis K. Meisel, 141 Prince Street, tel. 677 1340
Pleiades Gallery, 164 Mercer Street, tel. 266 9093
Sculpture Now, 138 Green Street, tel. 966 3066
Sonnabend Gallery, 420 West Broadway, tel. 966 6160
Vorpal Soho, 465 West Broadway, tel. 777 3939
Ward-Nasse, 178 Prince Street, tel. 925 6951
John Weber Gallery, 142 Green Street, tel. 966 6115

Opening times

With few exceptions Tues.–Sat. 10 a.m. to 5 or 6 p.m.

Photograph galleries

Exhibiting only photographs, either historical or contemporary.

Camera Club of New York
37 East 60th Street, tel. 223 9751
Open Mon.–Fri. 1–6 p.m.

Floating Foundation of Photography
Pier 40 (at end of Houston Street), tel. 242 3177
Open Thurs.–Sun. 12.30 p.m.–5.30 p.m.

Fourth Street Photo Gallery
67 East 4th Street, tel. 673 1021
Open Sun.–Thurs. 2–8 p.m., Fri. and Sat. 3–10 p.m.

Foto Gallery
492 Broome Street (SoHo), tel. 925 5612
Open Wed.–Sat. 1–6 p.m.

International Center of Photography
1130 Fifth Avenue (on 94th Street), tel. 860 1777
Open Wed.–Sun. 11 a.m.–5 p.m.

Neikrug Gallery
224 East 68th Street, tel. 268 7741
Open Wed.–Sat. 1–6 p.m.

Nikon House
620 Fifth Avenue (49th Street), tel. 586 3907
Open Tues.–Sat. 10 a.m.–5 p.m.

SoHo Photo
15 White Street, tel. 226 8571
Open Fri.–Sun. 1–6 p.m., Tues. 7–9 p.m.

Witkin
41 East 57th Street, tel. 355 1461
Open Tues.–Sat. 10 a.m.–5 p.m.

Getting to New York

Practically all visitors to New York now go by air. Only a few arrive in the last remaining transatlantic liner, Cunard's "Queen Elizabeth 2", or call in at New York in the course of a cruise.

Most international flights land at the J. F. Kennedy International Airport (see Airports) and discharge their passengers through the International Arrival Building. PanAm, TWA and British Airways have their own terminals.

Visitors arriving in New York will be well advised to come equipped with at least some American currency (dollar bills, coins) to cover small outgoings like tips, bus or taxi fares, telephone calls, etc. It is usually difficult and time-consuming to change large banknotes.

Hospitals

All major hospitals have casualty and emergency departments.

Lenox Hill Hospital, 100 East 77th Street, tel. 794 4567   Manhattan
Manhattan Eye, Ear and Throat Hospital, 210 East 64th Street, tel. 838 9200
New York Hospital, 70th Street (between First Avenue and York Avenue), tel. 794 3200
Roosevelt Hospital, 58th Street and Ninth Avenue, tel. 554 7000
St Clare's Hospital and Health Center, 415 West 51st Street, tel. 586 1500

See Emergency calls   Emergency calls

Hotels

New York has many hundreds of hotels, with over 100,000 beds in Manhattan alone; but it is still difficult at certain times to find accommodation, since the city attracts more than 17 million visitors a year, including two million from outside the United States. New York offers a wide range of accommodation for every taste and every purse, from luxury hotels to modest establishments in the less expensive parts of the city. Almost all the hotels listed below have rooms with private bath, air conditioning and colour television. Breakfast is never included in the room charge. Guests are not required to have breakfast in the hotel – many of the smaller hotels, indeed, do not serve breakfast – but can go out to a nearby coffee shop or cafeteria. Almost all hotels, particularly the larger ones, have one or more restaurants, with prices which vary in line with room charges. All hotels have safes in which money, jewellery and other valuables can be deposited. It is usually not necessary to leave your key at the reception desk every time you leave the hotel. Bills can be paid by traveller's cheque or credit card (American Express, Mastercharge, Visa, Diner's Club,

Carte Blanche). Room charges are subject to a tax which at the time of going to press is at the rate of 8¼%.
Advance reservation of rooms is strongly recommended.

In view of the continuing rise in hotel tariffs as a result of inflation the list of hotels given below does not attempt to show precise scales of charges. Hotels are listed in alphabetical order in four groups:

Luxury hotels (single rooms $80–$150, double rooms $105–$200).

Hotels with a high standard of amenity (single rooms $65–$100, double rooms $75–$130).

Good quality hotels (single rooms $45–$80, double rooms $60–$100).

Reasonably priced hotels (single rooms $30–$40, double rooms $40–$60).

Price categories

*Berkshire (420 rooms), 21 East 52nd Street, tel. 753 5800
*Carlyle (500 r.), 35 East 76th Street, tel. 744 1600
*Dorset (450 r.), 30 West 54th Street, tel. 247 7300
*Drake Swissotel (650 r.), 440 Park Avenue, tel. 421 0900
*Grand Hyatt (1400 r.), 42nd Street and Lexington Avenue, tel. 883 1234
*Halloran House (650 r.), 525 Lexington Avenue, tel. 755 4000
*Harley (900 r.), 212 East 42nd Street, tel. 490 8900
*Marriott's Essex House (720 r.), 160 Central Park South, tel. 247 0300
*Mayfair Regent (250 r.), 610 Park Avenue, tel. 288 0800
*Meridien (450 r.), 118 West 57th Street, tel. 245 5000
*New York Hilton (2100 r.), 1335 Avenue of the Americas, tel. 586 7000
*Palace (1100 r.), 455 Madison Avenue, tel. 888 7000
*Park Lane (650 r), 36 Central Park South, tel. 371 4000
*Pierre (700 r.), Fifth Avenue and 61st Street, tel. 838 8000
*Plaza (1000 r.), Fifth Avenue and 59th Street, tel. 759 3000
*Regency (500 r.), 540 Park Avenue, tel. 759 4100
*Sheraton Center (2000 r.), 811 Seventh Avenue, tel. 581 1000
*Sherry-Netherland (370 r.), 781 Fifth Avenue, tel. 355 2800
*St Regis Sheraton (550 r.), 2 East 55th Street, tel. 753 4500
*Tuscany (250 r.), 120 East 39th Street, tel. 686 1900
*United Nations Plaza (300 r.), 1 United Nations Plaza, tel. 355 3400
*Vista International (825 r.), 3 World Trade Center, tel. 938 9100
*Waldorf Astoria (1900 r.), Park Avenue and 50th Street, tel. 355 3000

Luxury hotels

American Stanhope (200 r), 995 Fifth Avenue, tel. 288 5800
Bedford (200 r.), 118 East 40th Street, tel. 697 4800
Doral Inn (700 r.), 541 Lexington Avenue, tel. 755 1200
Doral Park Avenue (200 r.), 70 Park Avenue, tel. 687 7050
Elysee (150 r.), 60 East 54th Street, tel. 753 1066
Gotham Nova Park (350 r.), 700 Fifth Avenue, tel. 307 1500
Inter-Continental (800 r.), 111 East 48th Street, tel. 755 5900

High amenity hotels

◀ *United Nations Plaza Hotel*

Entrance of Waldorf-Astoria Hotel

Plaza Hotel, with sculpture by Karl Bitter, "Abundance"

Loew's Summit (800 r.), Lexington Avenue and 51st Street,
tel. 752 7000
Middletowne (240 r.), 148 East 48th Street, tel. 755 3000
New York Sheraton (1600 r.), Seventh Avenue and
56th Street, tel. 247 8000
Roosevelt (1100 r.), Madison Avenue and 45th Street,
tel. 661 9600
San Carlos (150 r.), 150 East 50th Street, tel. 755 1800
Sheraton City Squire (720 r.), 790 Seventh Avenue,
tel. 581 3300
Sheraton Russell (175 r), 45 Park Avenue, tel. 685 7676
St Moritz (1000 r.), 50 Central Park South, tel. 755 5800
Warwick (500 r.), 65 West 54th Street, tel. 247 2700

Adams (300 r.) 2 East 86th Street, tel. 744 1800   Good quality hotels
Algonquin (200 r.), 59 West 44th Street, tel. 840 6800
Barbizon Plaza (800 r.), 106 Central Park South,
tel. 247 7000
Beverly (300 r.), 125 East 50th Street, tel. 753 2700
Blackstone (200 r.), 50 East 58th Street, tel. 355 4200
Executive (200 r.), 237 Madison Avenue, tel. 686 0300
Gorham (160 r.), 136 West 55th Street, tel. 245 1800
Gramercy Park (500 r.), Lexington Avenue and 21st Street,
tel. 475 4320
Holiday Inn-Coliseum (600 r.), 440 West 57th Street,
tel. 581 8100
Howard Johnson's Motor Lodge (300 r.), Eighth Avenue and
51st Street, tel. 581 4100
Kitano (100 r.), 66 Park Avenue, tel. 685 0022
Lexington (800 r.), 511 Lexington Avenue, tel. 755 4400
Mayflower (600 r.), Central Park West and 61st Street,
tel. 265 0060
Milford Plaza (1000 r.), 270 West 45th Street, tel. 869 3600
New York Statler (1700 r.), 401 Seventh Avenue, tel. 736 5000
Roger Smith (200 r.), 501 Lexington Avenue, tel. 755 1400
Royalton (200 r.), 44 West 44th Street, tel. 730 1344
Salisbury (320 r.), 123 West 57th Street, tel. 246 1300
Shoreham (200 r.), 33 West 55th Street, tel. 247 6700
Tudor (250 r.), 304 East 42nd Street, tel. 986 8800
Windsor (300 r.), 100 West 58th Street, tel. 265 2100
Wyndham (175 r.), 42 West 58th Street, tel. 753 3500

Allerton House for Women (400 r.), 130 East 57th Street,   Reasonably priced hotels
tel. 753 8841
Carter (700 r.), 250 West 43rd Street, tel. 947 6000
Century Paramount (700 r.), 235 West 46th Street,
tel. 764 5501
Diplomat (220 r.), 108 West 43rd Street, tel. 279 3707
Empire (600 r.), 63rd Street and Broadway, tel. 265 7400
Excelsior (300 r.), 45 West 81st Street, tel. 362 9200
George Washington (600 r.), Lexington Avenue and
23rd Street, tel. 475 1920
Mansfield (200 r.), 12 West 44th Street, tel. 682 5140
Martha Washington (women only: 500 r.),
30 East 30th Street, tel. 689 1900
Murray Hill (140 r.), 42 West 35th Street, tel. 947 0200
Penn Terminal (145 r.), 215 West 34th Street, tel. 947 5050
Pickwick Arms (400 r.), 250 East 51st Street, tel. 335 0300
Piccadilly (600 r.), 227 West 45th Street, tel. 246 6600

Prince George (1000 r.), 14 East 28th Street, tel. 532 7800
Seville (500 r.), Madison Avenue and 29th Street,
tel. 532 4100
Stanford (160 r.), 43 West 32nd Street, tel. 563 1480
Taft (1400 r.), 777 Seventh Avenue, tel. 247 4000
Wales (100 r.), 1295 Madison Avenue, tel. 876 6000

Insurance

It is essential to take out short-term health and accident
insurance when visiting the United States, since the costs of
medical treatment are high; and it is also advisable to have
baggage insurance and (particularly if you have booked a
package holiday) cancellation insurance. Arrangements can be
made through your travel agent or insurance company; many
companies running package holidays now include insurance
as part of the deal.

Within the United States foreign visitors can effect insurance
through American International Underwriters, 1225 Connecticut Avenue, NW, Suite 414, Washington, D.C. 20036. (UK
address: 120 Fenchurch Street, London WC3M 5BP).

Jazz

See Night Life

Language

British (and other) visitors may find it helpful to be reminded of
some of the differences between American and British usage.

British	American
autumn	fall
bill	check
billion – 1000 million (now widely accepted in Britain, where traditionally a billion was a million million)	billion
biscuit	cracker, cookie
bonnet	hood (of car)
boot	trunk (of car)
braces	suspenders
caravan	trailer
carry-out	"to go" (in cafeteria, etc.)
cinema	movie (theater)
cloakroom	checkroom
cupboard	closet
dustbin	garbage can
first floor	second floor
flat	apartment
football	soccer
fortnight	two weeks
"gents" (lavatory)	men's room

graduation (university, etc.)	commencement
ground floor	first floor
handbag	purse
label	sticker
"ladies" (lavatory)	ladies' room, powder room
lavatory	rest room
lavatory (roadside)	comfort station
lift	elevator
lorry	truck
luggage	baggage
maize	corn
nappy	diaper
open square	plaza
pavement	sidewalk
personal call (on telephone)	person to person call
petrol	gas, gasoline
post	mail
post code	zip code
queue	(stand in) line
(railway) line, platform	track
refrigerator	icebox
return ticket	round trip ticket
reversed charge	collect (on telephone)
ring (up)	call (on telephone)
scone	biscuit
second floor	third floor
shop	store
single ticket	one way ticket
spanner	wrench
subway	underpass
summer time	daylight saving time
surname	last name
tap	faucet
tin	can (e.g. of food)
tram	streetcar
trousers	pants
trunk call	long distance call
underground	subway
viewpoint, viewing platform	observatory
Whitsun	Pentecost

It is perhaps worth a special reminder that in multi-storey buildings the Americans begin counting the storeys from street level, so that the American first floor is the British ground floor, the American second floor is the British first floor, and so on.

Libraries and archives

The principal New York libraries, apart from the Public Library (see A to Z, New York Public Library), are the following:

Libraries

Frick Art Reference Library
10 East 71st Street
Art

Grolier Club
47 East 60th Street
Bibliophile editions

Institute of Fine Arts
1 East 78th Street, tel. 988 5500
Art

Museum of the City of New York
See A to Z

New York Historical Society
See A to Z

New York Law Institute
53 East 79th Street, tel. 732 8720
Law

New York Society Library
53 East 79th Street, tel. 288 6900
A subscription lending library founded in 1754

Pierpont Morgan Library
See A to Z

Walter Hampden Memorial Library
16 Gramercy Square South, tel. 228 7610
The theatre

For students and teaching
staff only

Bobst Library, New York University
70 Washington Square South, tel. 598 2450

Columbia University Libraries, on University campus,
tel. 280 3533

There are also numerous specialised libraries for particular
disciplines, and each college has a library for its own students.

Archives

Library and Museum of the Performing Arts
See A to Z, Lincoln Center

Leo Baeck Institute
129 East 73rd Street, tel. 744 6400
German-Jewish history

Schomburg Center for Research in Black Culture
See A to Z

Zionist Archives and Library
515 Park Avenue, tel. 753 2167

Opening times

Opening times vary, and some of the libraries and archives are
not open every day. It is advisable to check by telephone that
a particular establishment will be open before visiting it.

Lost property

Airports

J. F. Kennedy Airport: apply to the airline concerned. If you lose
something within the airport tel. 656 4120.
La Guardia Airport: tel. 476 5128 or apply to the airline
concerned.
Newark Airport: tel. (201) 961 2235 or apply to the airline.

Taxis

Tel. 825 0416. If the article has not turned up within 48 hours
tel. 374 5084.

Tel. 625 6200.	Subway
In Manhattan and Bronx tel. 690 9543. In Brooklyn, Queens and Staten Island tel. 625 6200.	Buses
Grand Central Station: tel. 340 2571. Pennsylvania Station: tel. 239 6193.	Railway
New York Port Authority Bus Terminal, tel. 466 7000, ext. 219; Sat., Sun. and public holidays, tel. 564 9523, ext. 219.	Country buses

Markets

Ninth Avenue, between 39th and 54th Streets Union Square, April–December, only Wed. and Sat. 7 a.m.–6 p.m.	Vegetables
86th Street, between Second and Third Avenues	German products
14th Street, W of Seventh Avenue	Spanish products
Annex Flea Market, 200 West 20th Street Antiques Market, 137 Ludlow Street Manhattan Art and Antiques Center, 1050 Second Avenue (56th Street)	Flea markets

Movies

See Cinemas

Museums

Museums are listed in alphabetical order.

Abigail Adams Smith Museum
421 East 61st Street (a building dating from 1799)
Open Mon.–Fri. 10 a.m.–4 p.m.

Afro Arts Cultural Center
2191 Adam C. Powell Jr Boulevard
Open daily 9 a.m.–8 p.m.; admission free
Bronze, stone and wood sculpture, pictures and artefacts of all
kinds from North, East, Central, West and Southern Africa.

American Museum of Immigration
See A to Z, Statue of Liberty

American Museum of Natural History
See A to Z

Asia House Gallery
See A to Z

Bronx Museum of the Arts
Rotunda in Bronx County Courthouse
Grand Concourse
Open Sat. and Sun. 10 a.m.–4.30 p.m.

Practical Information

Brooklyn Children's Museum
See A to Z

Brooklyn Museum
See A to Z

China House Gallery
See A to Z

Chinatown Museum
See A to Z, Chinatown

Cloisters Museum
See A to Z

Cooper-Hewitt Museum
See A to Z

Dyckman House
See A to Z

Fire Department Museum
104 Duane Street
Open Tues.–Fri. 9 a.m.–4 p.m., Sat. and Sun. 9 a.m.–2 p.m.;
closed on public holidays

Fraunces Tavern
See A to Z

Frick Collection
See A to Z

Fort Wadsworth Military Museum
Fort Tomkins, Staten Island
Open Mon., Thurs., Fri. and Sun. 1 4 p.m., Sat. 10 a.m.–4 p.m.

Guggenheim Museum
See A to Z

Hall of Fame for Great Americans
University Avenue and West 181st Street, Bronx
Open daily 10 a.m.–5 p.m.

Hispanic Society of America Museum
See A to Z

International Center of Photography
1130 Fifth Avenue
Open Tues.–Fri. noon–8 p.m., Sat. and Sun. noon–6 p.m.

Jacques Marchais Center of Tibetan Art
See A to Z

Jewish Museum
See A to Z

Metropolitan Museum of Art
See A to Z

Morris Jumel Mansion
See A to Z

Museo del Barrio
See A to Z

Museum of American Folk Art
See A to Z

Museum of the American Indian
See A to Z

Museum of Broadcasting
See A to Z

Museum of Bronx History
3266 Bainbridge Avenue
Open Sat. 10 a.m.–4 p.m., Sun. 1–5 p.m.

Museum of the City of New York
See A to Z

Museum of Holography
See A to Z

Museum of Modern Art
See A to Z

New Museum
See A to Z

New York Experience
See A to Z, Rockefeller Center

New York Historical Society
See A to Z

New York Public Transit Exhibit
Old Subway Station,
Boerum Place and Schermerhorn Street, Brooklyn
Open daily 10 a.m.–4 p.m.

Old Merchant's House
See A to Z

Pierpont Morgan Library
See A to Z

Poe Cottage
See A to Z

Police Academy Museum
235 East 20th Street
Open Mon.–Fri. 1–4 p.m.

Richmondtown Restoration
See A to Z

Nicolas Roerich Museum
319 West 197th Street
Open Sun.–Fri. 2–4 p.m.
Documents by and on Roerich; Asian art.

Schomburg Center for Research in Black Culture
See A to Z

Sea Air Space Museum in the former aircraft-carrier "Intrepid"
Intrepid Square Pier 86, West 46th Street, Twelfth Avenue
Open daily 10 a.m.–6 or 8 p.m.

Songwriters Hall of Fame
See A to Z

South Street Seaport Museum
See A to Z

Staten Island Historical Museum
See A to Z, Richmondtown Restoration

Staten Island Institute of Arts and Sciences
75 Stuyvesant Place, St George
Open Tues.–Sat. 10 a.m.–5 p.m., Sun. 2–5 p.m.

Studio Museum of Harlem
See A to Z

Theodore Roosevelt Birthplace
See A to Z

Ukrainian Museum
See A to Z

Van Cortlandt Mansion
See A to Z

Whitney Museum of American Art
See A to Z

Yeshiva University Museum
500 West 185th Street
Open Tues.–Thurs. 11 a.m.–5 p.m., Sun. noon–6 p.m.

Music

Opera

New York has two major opera companies and a number of
smaller companies which give only occasional performances.
The two principal opera-houses are part of the Lincoln Center
(See A to Z).

Metropolitan Opera House
Broadway (between 61st and 66th Streets), tel. 580 9830
Subway: 66th Street (line 1), 59th Street (lines A, B, D, AA,
CC)
Buses: 5, 7, 30, 104
Season: end September to April. Performances Mon.–Fri.
(evenings), Sat. (afternoon and evening); closed Sun.
The repertoire is relatively small, and includes hardly any
modern works, which appeal to the Met's audiences less than
the operas of Wagner, Verdi, Puccini, etc.; but since the Met,
like other cultural institutions in New York, is privately run and
must cover 70% of its outgoings from box office receipts it has
to have regard to box office appeal.
The Metropolitan Opera, founded in 1883, was based until
1966 in its old opera-house (now demolished) on Broadway,
between 39th and 40th Streets. The new Metropolitan Opera

House in the Lincoln Center, designed by the New York architect Wallace K. Harrison and opened in the autumn of 1966, has exactly the same number of seats (3600) as the old house.

During the season the Met puts on seven performances every week.

New York City Opera

New York State Theater, Lincoln Center. Transport details as for Metropolitan Opera House.

Season: July–November.

Seven performances a week; closed Mon.

Founded in 1943, the New York City Opera was housed for the first 20 years of its existence in the New York City Center at 131 West 51st Street. It took over its present premises in the Lincoln Center in 1964. It is directed by the celebrated diva Beverly Sills, now retired from her career as a singer. The house can accommodate an audience of 2800. The City Opera, like the Met, has a conventional repertoire, but it does make more attempt to present contemporary operas, particularly by American composers – though it must be said that not all its efforts in this direction have been equally successful.

The City Opera, like the Met, gives seven performances a week. It is closed on Mondays but regularly gives two performances on Saturdays; it sometimes gives two performances on Sundays as well, in which event there are no performances on Tuesday or Thursday. Tickets cost less than for the Metropolitan Opera, but the City Opera does not feature the great international stars.

Ballet

New York is often called the ballet capital of the world, by virtue not only of its own great ballet ensembles and its many smaller companies but also of the visiting companies from the United States and many other countries which perform in the city.

Among directors of ballet and dance companies who have worked in New York have been such outstanding choreographers as Jerome Robbins, Robert Joffrey, Martha Graham, Arthur Mitchell and Alwyn Nikolais etc. With the exception of the two principal companies, the American Ballet and the New York City Ballet, the New York companies concentrate mostly on the modern expressive style of dancing. The following companies give regular performances:

American Ballet Theater
Metropolitan Opera House, Lincoln Center, tel. 580 9830
Season: mid April to mid June.

New York City Ballet
New York State Theater, Lincoln Center, tel. 877 4700
Season: beginning of May to beginning of July, November to February.

Alvin Ailey American Dance Theater
City Center, 131 West 55th Street, tel. 246 8989
Season: first half of May, second half of November.

Joffrey Ballet
City Center, 131 West 55th Street, tel. 246 8989
Season: March, October.

Palladium

Madison Square Garden

Paul Taylor Dance Company
City Center, 131 West 55th Street, tel. 246 8989
Season: April.

Other good dance companies, with no regular season, are the
following:
Merce Cunningham Dance Company, tel. 355 8240
Dance Theater of Harlem, tel. 690 2800
Eliot Feld Ballet, tel. 873 5493
Martha Graham Dance Company, tel. 838 5886
Erik Hawkins Dance Company, tel. 255 6698
Murray Louis Dance Company, tel. 777 1120
Nikolais Dance Theater, tel. 777 1120
Twyla Tharp Dance Foundation, tel. 955 2590

During the main season (October–April) there are some 150   Concerts
concerts and recitals every week in New York, from the
concerts given four times a week (Tues., Thurs., Fri. and Sat.)
by the New York Philharmonic Orchestra in the Lincoln Center
and the concerts by other major US and foreign orchestras, by
way of choral events and chamber music to a host of solo
recitals by pianists and singers.

Abraham Goodman Hall, 129 West 67th Street, tel. 362 8719   Concert halls
Alice Tully Hall, Lincoln Center, tel. 362 1911
Avery Fisher Hall, Lincoln Center, tel. 874 2424
Carnegie Hall, 154 West 57th Street, tel. 247 1350

Metropolitan Museum, Fifth Avenue and 82nd Street   Regular concert series
New School of Social Research, 66 West 12th Street
YM-YWHA, 1395 Lexington Avenue (92nd Street)

The New York jazz scene is so varied and changes so rapidly   Jazz concerts
that any information given here would be quickly out of date.
The best plan for jazz enthusiasts, therefore, is to ring the Jazz
Line (tel. 423 0488) for the latest news of what's on.
Important jazz events are sometimes held in the concert hall
mentioned above.

See Night life   Jazz clubs

Well-known rock bands and singers perform in the following   Rock concerts
theatres:

Palladium
112 East 14th Street (near Union Square), tel. 249 8870

Madison Square Garden
Seventh Avenue and 32nd Street, tel. 564 4400

See Night life   Rock clubs

There are recitals of church music in many New York churches,   Church music
mainly at Christmas and Easter but by no means only then. They
are listed in the Saturday edition of the "New York Times".

Concerts and opera performances (admission free) are given by   Concerts in the parks
the New York Philharmonic and the Metropolitan Opera during
the month of June in Central Park and in parks in the other four
New York boroughs. Information: tel. 755 4100 or 580 8700.

Newspapers and periodicals

In spite of its population of 7 million New York has only three dailies:

The "New York Times", the most respected American newspaper, appears seven times a week. On weekdays it runs to between 72 and 124 pages, on Sundays to between 300 and 500.

The "Daily News", the American morning newspaper with the largest circulation, also appears seven times a week.

The "New York Post", America's oldest surviving newspaper, appears six times a week.

Even the strictly regional newspaper "USA Today" is now obtainable in New York.

For information about events in New York the following weeklies are useful:
"New Yorker" (Monday)
"New York Magazine" (Monday)
"Village Voice" (Wednesday).

Night life

Bars	Elaine's, 1703 Second Avenue
	Friday's, 1152 First Avenue
	Green Tree Hungarian Restaurant, 1034 Amsterdam Avenue
	Hoexter's Market Restaurant, 1442 Third Avenue
	Marvin Gardens, 2274 Broadway (82nd Street)
	The Libary, 2475 Broadway (92nd Street)
	West End Café, 2911 Broadway (113th Street)
Cabaret shows	Once Upon a Stove, 325 Third Avenue (25th Street), tel. 683 0044
Night clubs and discos	Adam's Apple, 1117 First Avenue (61st Street)
	Applause, 360 Lexington Avenue (40th Street)
	Barbizon Plaza Library (in Barbizon Plaza Hotel), 106 Central Park South (59th Street)
	Regine's, 502 Park Avenue (59th Street)
	Roxy, 515 West 18th Street (bring your roller skates)
Jazz clubs	Arthur's Tavern, 57 Grove Street (Greenwich Village)
	Cookery, 21 University Place (Greenwich Village)
	Eddie Condon's, 144 West 54th Street
	Fat Tuesday's, 190 Third Avenue (17th Street)
	Gregory's, 1149 First Avenue (63rd Street)
	Jazzmania Society, 40 West 27th Street
	Jimmy Ryan's, 154 West 54th Street
	Kelly's Village West, 46 Bedford Street
	Michael's Pub, 211 East 55th Street
	Red Blazer, Too, 1576 Third Avenue (88th Street)
	Seventh Avenue South, 21 Seventh Avenue South

Sweet Basil, 88 Seventh Avenue South
Village Gate, 160 Bleecker Street (Greenwich Village)

Back Fence, 155 Bleecker Street (Greenwich Village)   Rock clubs
Bottom Line, 15 West 4th Street (Greenwich Village)
CBGB, 315 Bowery (East Village)
Great Gildersleeves, 331 Bowery (East Village)
Mudd Club, 77 Water Street
Other End, 149 Bleecker Street (Greenwich Village)
Rocker Room, 1 East 48th Street

See Music   Rock concerts

Postal services

The US Post Office is responsible only for postal services.
The telephone and telegraph services (see entries) are run by
private enterprise.

Letters within the United States: 20 cents for the first ounce,   Postage rates
plus 17 cents for each additional ounce.
Air mail letters to Europe: 40 cents for each half ounce.
Postcards: 28 cents.
Stamps are most conveniently bought in a post office.

In midtown Manhattan: Post offices
General Post Office, Eighth Avenue and 33rd Street
Grand Central post office, Lexington Avenue and 45th Street
Times Square post office, 340 West 42nd Street
Rockefeller Center post office, RCA Building
Franklin D. Roosevelt post office, 909 Third Avenue (55th
Street)
Bryant post office, 23 West 43rd Street
Empire State post office, 19 West 33rd Street
Columbus Circle post office, 27 West 60th Street.

There are also post offices in Macy's and Bloomingdale's
department stores (see Department stores).

Usually Mon.–Fri. 8.30 a.m.–6 p.m., Sat. 9 a.m.–noon. The   Opening times
General Post Office is open all the time.
After closing time, stamps can be bought from coin-operated
machines.

Poste restante letters should be marked "General Delivery".   Poste restante

This is a five-figure number following the two-letter abbrevia-   Zip code (post code)
tion for the state: e.g. New York, NY 10017. The last figures of
the number vary according to the district.

These are painted blue, with the legend "US Mail" in white.   Letter-boxes

See Telephone   Telephone

See Telegrams   Telegrams

Public holidays

With the exception of Easter Day, Christmas Day and New Year's Day many shops remain open on official holidays, though banks, the Stock Exchange, government offices and schools are closed. On Christmas festivals (Easter, Christmas) there is no extra public holiday.

Most official holidays vary slightly from year to year, being fixed for the Monday before or after the actual day in order to make a long weekend.

Statutory public holidays

New Year's Day (1 January); Washington's Birthday (third Monday in February); Easter Day; Memorial or Decoration Day (last Monday in May); Independence Day (4 July); Labor Day (first Monday in September); Columbus Day (second Monday in October); Veteran's Day or Armistice Day (11 November); Thanksgiving Day (fourth Thursday in November); Christmas Day (25 December).

Radio and television

New York has seven television stations and some 50 radio stations, some of them operating 24 hours a day. With the exception of one television station, WNET, and two radio stations, WNYC and WBAI, they are all commercial, financing their operations by the sale of transmission time and advertising spots.

Radio

There are few live programmes on American radio. Most stations make much use of records and tapes, sometimes specialising in a particular kind of music (classical, jazz, rock). Some transmit programmes directed at particular ethnic groups; others send out news all day long.

Television

Some television stations admit an audience to the transmission or recording of certain programmes. For information apply to the following stations:

WABC (Channel 7), 1330 Avenue of the Americas, tel. 581 7777

WCBS (Channel 2), 51 West 52nd Street, tel. 975 2476

WNBC (Channel 4), 30 Rockefeller Plaza, tel. 664 4444

WNET (Channel 13), 356 West 58th Street, tel. 560 2000

WNEW (Channel 5), 205 East 67th Street, tel. 535 1000

WOR (Channel 9), 1440 Broadway, tel. 764 6683

WPIX (Channel 11). 220 East 42nd Street, tel. 949 1100

Programme information

Television programmes and the programmes of the principal radio stations are given daily in the newspapers.

Railway and bus stations

Railways

Since the railway plays relatively little part in the transport network of the United States, visitors to New York will have little occasion to travel by train, except perhaps to the suburbs and between New York, Washington and Philadelphia.

Passenger services are run (with large government subsidies) by the Amtrak corporation, to which practically all the private rail companies have leased their stations, track and rolling stock.

New York has two main-line railway stations:

Grand Central Terminal, 42nd Street and Park Avenue
Information: tel. 736 4545
Surban services and services to the northern and western United States.

Penn Station, 33rd Street and Seventh Avenue
Information: tel. 736 4545
Services run by the Long Island Railroad (tel. 739 4200) and services to the southern and western United States.

The main competition to air and rail services for long-distance travel in the United States is provided by country-wide bus services, which are cheaper than travelling by rail. Almost all the traffic is carried by two companies, Greyhound and Trailways.

Long-distance bus services

All buses depart from and arrive at the central bus station:
Port Authority Bus Terminal, Eighth Avenue (40th–42nd Streets)
Information: tel. 564 8484
Greyhound: tel. 594 2000
Trailways: tel. 730 7460

The bus companies offer short-term season tickets (Greyhound's "Ameripass" and Trailways' "Eaglepass") allowing unlimited travel on all their services for a week, two weeks or a month. For those who want to see America by bus this is much cheaper than buying a series of separate tickets.

Rent-a-Car

See Car hire

Restaurants

New York is reliably reported to have almost 15,000 restaurants, from the most exclusive establishments to the most modest coffee shops and cafeterias. There is a wide price range, from the luxury restaurants, where the standard meal may cost about 80 dollars a head, to the smaller places, where a satisfying meal can be had for a few dollars. Lunch is almost always cheaper than dinner. In reading the menus, which are almost always posted up outside the restaurant, remember to allow for tax at 8·25% and a tip of perhaps 15% of the bill. The prices of drinks are not usually posted up, but wine tends to be dear. There is, however, no obligation to order drinks. Iced water is always supplied free of charge.
Almost every national cuisine in the world is represented in New York. Thus in 55th and 56th Streets, between Fifth Avenue and the Avenue of the Americas, there is a choice of

Japanese, Chinese, Korean, Italian and French restaurants. The cheapest Chinese food – and frequently the best – is to be found in modest establishments in Chinatown. For Near Eastern cuisine the best area is between 28th and 32nd Streets, on both sides of Lexington Avenue, where there are many Lebanese and Syrian restaurants. French and Italian restaurants – the most numerous of the foreign restaurants apart from the Chinese – are mainly to be found on East Side, where there is some competition between the traditional *haute cuisine* and the now fashionable *nouvelle cuisine*.

These are perhaps the more popular of the foreign cuisines which can be sampled in New York, but there are numerous other restaurants offering Argentinian, Brazilian, British, Czech, Danish, Filipino, Greek, Indian, Mexican, Persian, Russian, Thai, Turkish, Ukrainian and West Indian food – to mention only a few.

In many restaurants, particularly those in the higher price ranges, it is necessary to book a table by telephone.

All New York restaurants are listed in the "Yellow Pages" telephone directory. The following is only a brief selection. The list does not include hotel restaurants. (All the larger hotels have restaurants, often more than one.)
The various types of cuisine are distinguished as follows:

A   = American
C   = Chinese
F   = French
FR = fish restaurant
G   = German
I   = Italian
J   = Japanese
K   = Korean
R   = Russian
Sp = Spanish
Sw = Swiss

The letters *L* (luxury) and *E* (expensive) give some indication of price level.

East Side of Manhattan
(42nd–86th Streets)

Argenteuil (F, *E*), 253 East 53rd Street, tel. 753 9273
Bavarian Inn (G), 232 East 86th Street, tel. 650 1056
Brussels (F, *L*), 115 East 54th Street, tel. 758 0457
Chalet Suisse (Sw), 6 East 48th Street, tel. 355 0855
Cheval Blanc (F, *E*), 145 East 45th Street, tel. 986 4729
Clos Normand (F), 560 Lexington Avenue, tel. 753 3348
Christ Cella (A), 160 East 46th Street, tel. 697 2479
Four Seasons (A, *E*), 99 East 65th Street, tel. 754 9494
Gavroche (F), 222 East 58th Street, tel. 838 0279
Gian Marino (I), 221 East 58th Street, tel. 752 1696
Giovanni (I), 66 East 55th Street, tel. 753 1230
Gold Coin (C), 835 Second Avenue (44th Street),
tel. 697 1515
La Bibliothèque (F), 341 East 43rd Street, tel. 661 5757
La Côte Basque (F, *E*), 5 East 55th Street, tel. 688 6525
La Grenouille (F), 3 East 52nd Street, tel. 532 1495
La Rôtisserie (F), 153 East 52nd Street, tel. 795 1685
L'Olivier (F), 248 East 49th Street, tel. 385 1810
Lutèce (F, *L*), 240 East 50th Street, tel. 532 2225
Mario's Villa d'Este (I), 58 East 56th Street, tel. 759 4025
Mitsukoshi (J), 465 Park Avenue (57th Street), tel. 935 6444

Oyster Bar (FR), Grand Central Station, tel. 532 3888
Peng Teng (C), 219 East 44th Street, tel. 682 8050
Pronto (I), 33 East 60th Street, tel. 421 8157
Saito (J), 305 East 46th Street, tel. 795 8897
Shinbashi (J), 280 Park Avenue (48th Street), tel. 661 3915
Sichuan Pavilion (C), 322 East 44th Street, tel. 986 3775
Uncle Tai (C), 1059 Third Avenue (63rd Street), tel. 752 9065

A la Fourchette (F), 342 West 46th Street, tel. 245 9744
Abruzzi (I), 37 West 56th Street, tel. 489 8110
Alfredo (I), 240 Central Park South, tel. 246 7050
Brittany du Soir (F), 800 Ninth Avenue (53rd Street),
tel. 265 4820
Café de la Paix (F), 50 Central Park South, tel. 755 5800
Cuisines of China (C), 40 West 53rd Street, tel. 246 0770
Carlos 2 (FR), 36 West 48th Street, tel. 869 8366
Du Midi (F), 311 West 48th Street, tel. 582 6689
Fontana di Trevi (I), 151 West 57th Street, tel. 247 5683
French Shack (F), 65 West 55th Street, tel. 246 5126
Fuji (J), 238 West 56th Street, tel. 245 8594
Gallagher's Steak House (A), 228 West 52nd Street,
tel. 245 5336
Izakaya (J), 43 West 54th Street, tel. 765 4683
Joe's Pier 52 (FR), 144 West 52nd Street, tel. 245 6652
Kyoto Steak House (J), 148 West 46th Street, tel. 265 2344
La Caravelle (F), 33 West 55th Street, tel. 586 4252
La Grillade (F), 845 Eighth Avenue (51st Street), tel. 265 1610
La Strada (I), 134 West 46th Street, tel. 245 2660
Le Biarritz (F), 325 West 57th Street, tel. 245 9467
Les Pyrénées (F), 251 West 51st Street, tel. 246 0044
Luchow's (G), 1633 Broadway, tel. 582 4697
Mamma Leone (I), 239 West 48th Street, tel. 586 5151
Miyako (J), 20 West 56th Street, tel. 265 3177
Orsini (I), 41 West 56th Street, tel. 757 1698
Pearl's (C), 38 West 48th Street, tel. 486 1010
Rainbow Room (F, L), 30 Rockefeller Plaza, tel. 757 9090
Romeo Salta (I, E), 30 West 56th Street, tel. 246 5772
Russian Tearoom (R), 150 West 57th Street, tel. 265 0947
Sacred Cow Steak House (A), 228 West 72nd Street,
tel. 873 4067
Sardi (A), 234 West 44th Street, tel. 221 8440
Seafare of the Aegean (FR), 25 West 56th Street, tel. 581 0540
Stouffer's Top of the Six (A), 666 Fifth Avenue (53rd Street),
tel. 757 6662
Swiss Center Restaurant (Sw), 4 West 49th Street,
tel. 247 6545
Vesuvio (I), 163 West 48th Street, tel. 245 6138
Wally's (A), 224 West 49th Street, tel. 582 0460

West Side of Manhattan
(42nd–73rd Streets)

Angelo (I), 146 Mulberry Street, tel. 966 1277
Bianchi and Margherita, 186 West 4th Street, tel. 242 2756
Buchbinder's (A), 375 Third Avenue (27th Street),
tel. 683 6500
Food (A), 127 Prince Street, tel. 473 8790
Fraunces Tavern (A), Broad and Pearl Streets, tel. 269 0144
Giambelli (I), 228 Madison Avenue (38th Street),
tel. 685 2727
Hisae (FR), 35 Cooper Square, tel. 228 6886
La Colombe d'Or (F), 134 East 26th Street, tel. 689 0666
La Gamelle (F), 59 Grand Street, tel. 431 6695
La Gauloise (F), 502 Avenue of the Americas, tel. 691 1363

Manhattan
below 42nd Street

O'Henry's (A), 345 Avenue of the Americas, tel. 242 2000
One Fifth (A), 1 Fifth Avenue, tel. 260 3434
Pete's Tavern (A), 129 East 18th Street, tel. 473 7676
Raffaela's (I), 134 West Houston Street, tel. 982 0464
Sevilla (Sp), 62 Charles Street, tel. 929 3189
Spain (Sp), 113 West 13th Street, tel. 929 9580
Toots Shor (A), 233 West 33rd Street, tel. 279 8150
Windows on the World (A, *E*), World Trade Center,
tel. 938 1111

Shopping

Department stores	See Department stores
Markets	See Markets
Specialist shops	The following is a selection of specialist shops.
Chocolates	Godiva Chocolatier, 701 Fifth Avenue Teuscher Chocolates of Switzerland, 620 Fifth Avenue and 25 East 61st Street
Coins	Deak-Perera Fifth Avenue, 630 Fifth Avenue
Fashion houses	Bergdorf-Goodman Fifth Avenue and 58th Street Open Sat. 10 a.m.–6 p.m.; closed Sun. Henri Bendel 10 West 57th Street Open Mon.–Sat. 10 a.m.–5.30 p.m.; closed Sun.
Fashion for the family	Alexander's, Lexington Avenue and 58th Street Brooks Brothers, 346 Madison Avenue (44th Street) Kreeger and Sons, 16 West 46th Street Lord and Taylor, Fifth Avenue and 39th Street Saks Fifth Avenue, Fifth Avenue and 50th Street
Fashion for women	Charivari for Women, 2707 Broadway (84th Street) Lerner Shops, 17 West 34th Street; and seven other shops in Manhattan Plymouth, 30 Rockefeller Plaza; and seven other shops in Manhattan
Fashion for women and men	Barney's, Seventh Avenue and 17th Street Riding High, 1143 First Avenue (between 62nd and 63rd Streets)
Fashion for men	Charivari for Men, 2339 Broadway (85th Street) F. R. Tripler and Co., Madison Avenue and 46th Street Wallachs, Empire State Building and 555 Fifth Avenue (46th Street)
Flowers	Renny, 27 East 62nd Street and 251 East 62nd Street
Furs	Emilio Gucci Furs, 333 Seventh Avenue, 4th floor Furland Express, 330 Seventh Avenue (29th Street), 9th floor

The best known jewellers are concentrated in the area of Fifth Avenue and 57th Street:
Bulgari, Fifth Avenue and 61st Street
Cartier, 653 Fifth Avenue (52nd Street)
Aaron Faber, 666 Fifth Avenue (53rd Street)
Michael C. Fina, 580 Fifth Avenue (47th Street)
Fortunoff, 681 Fifth Avenue (55th Street)
Jerry Grant, 137 East 57th Street
Lambert Brothers, 545 Madison Avenue (55th Street)
Mikimoto (America), 608 Fifth Avenue (42nd Street)
Spritzer and Fuhrmann, 5 East 57th Street, 4th floor
Tiffany and Co., 727 Fifth Avenue (57th Street)
Van Cleef and Arpels, 744 Fifth Avenue (57th Street)
David Webb, 7 East 57th Street
Harry Winston, 718 Fifth Avenue (56th Street)

Jewellers

Alfred Dunhill of London, 620 Fifth Avenue (50th Street)
Nat Sherman, 711 Fifth Avenue (55th Street)

Pipes and smokers' articles

Barnes and Noble, Sales Annex, 128 Fifth Avenue (18th Street)
Barnes and Noble, 600 Fifth Avenue (48th Street)
Colony Records, 1619 Broadway (49th Street)
Sam Goody, 51 West 51st Street
Sam Goody, 235 West 49th Street
Sam Goody, 666 Third Avenue
King Karol, 126 West 42nd Street
King Karol, 1500 Broadway (Times Square)
King Karol, 940 Third Avenue
Record Hunter, 507 Fifth Avenue (42nd Street)

Records

United Nations Postal Administration,
First Avenue and 46th Street
UN stamps for collectors

Stamps

F. A. O. Schwarz, 745 Fifth Avenue (55th Street)

Toys

Sightseeing tours

A number of organisations conduct guided walks:

On foot

Friends of Cast-Iron Architecture
235 East 87th Street, tel. 427 2488
Walks in spring and autumn through parts of the city, particularly in SoHo, where there are 19th c. cast-iron buildings.

Holidays in New York
152 West 58th Street, tel. 765 2515
Walks conducted by a knowledgeable guide, mainly in southern Manhattan (Chinatown, Little Italy, SoHo, Greenwich Village).

Municipal Art Society
457 Madison Avenue, tel. 935 3960
Guided walks from May to the beginning of September introducing the participants to the architecture of New York and changes in the face of the city.

Museum of American Folk Art
49 West 53rd Street, tel. 581 2475
Visits by small groups to New York buildings or houses of particular interest are organised at irregular intervals.

Museum of the City of New York
103rd Street and Fifth Avenue, tel. 534 1672
Walks through different parts of Manhattan on Sunday afternoons from April to October.

By bus

Crossroads Sightseeing
701 Seventh Avenue, tel. 581 2828
Whole-day and half-day tours of Manhattan.

Gray Line
900 Eighth Avenue, tel. 397 2600
A programme of ten tours of Manhattan, lasting from $2\frac{1}{2}$ to $8\frac{1}{2}$ hours.

Harlem Renaissance Tours
228 East 125th Street, tel. 212 3316
Conducted tours of Harlem.

Manhattan Sightseeing
150 West 49th Street, tel. 245 6641
Ten half-day and whole-day trips (prior reservation).

New York Big Apple Tours
162 West 65th Street, tel. 582 6339
A programme of 15 tours.

Penny Sightseeing Co.
303 West 42nd Street, tel. 247 2860
This firm, run by blacks, organises three-hour tours of Harlem from March to November (Mon. and Thurs. 10 a.m., Sat. 1 p.m.). Prior reservation required.

Short Line Tours
166 West 46th Street, tel. 354 5122
A programme of eight day and evening tours of Manhattan.

Sightseeing cruises

Circle Line, tel. 563 3200
Three-hour sightseeing cruises around Manhattan, departing from Pier 83 (foot of West 43rd Street). Beginning of April to mid September, every 45 minutes from 9.45 a.m.

Boat excursions

See Boat excursions

Ferries

See Ferries

Helicopter trips

Island Helicopters, tel. 683 4575
Sightseeing flights lasting 5–7, 10–12, 15–17 or 30 minutes, daily 9 a.m.–5 p.m. Departure from Heliport, East River (end of East 34th Street).

Special interests

There are a variety of specialised programmes, some of them tailored to individual requirements. To avoid unpleasant surprises, enquire about cost in advance.

Adventure on a Shoestring, Inc.
300 West 53rd Street, tel. 265 2663
Unusual aspects of the life and people of New York.

Art Tours of Manhattan, Inc.
33 East 22nd Street, tel. 254 7682
Guided tours of museums, galleries, the artists' quarter of SoHo
and artists' studios.

Backstage on Broadway
228 West 47th Street, tel. 575 8065
Behind the scenes of a Broadway show under the guidance of
an actor.

Hello New York
430 East 86th Street, tel. 861 1323
Conducted tours by bus of the principal sights.

Tour and Study
1501 Broadway, tel. 944 9110
Sightseeing tours for those interested in particular fields.

Tours of Jewish New York
180 East 79th Street, tel. 628 2244
Four tours (not run every day) introducing visitors to the life of
New York Jews.

Young Visitors
30 West 70th Street, tel. 595 8100
Tours for children and student groups, introducing them to the
history of New York and the ethnic composition of its
population.

Sport

New York offers endless scope for every kind of sport and
recreation. Anglers and golfers are catered for in the Bronx,
Brooklyn, Queens and Staten Island; but the main centre of
sporting activity in New York is Central Park (see A to Z) in the
heart of Manhattan. Here there are facilities for roller skating
and ice skating, riding, cycling, rowing and playing tennis. (In
addition, there are many tennis courts, both public and private,
in all parts of the city.)
For information about sports facilities and particular sporting
events telephone 755 4100.

Some of the principal sports grounds are listed below.

N. Y. Mets, Shea Stadium, Flushing (Queens), tel. 672 3000   Baseball
N. Y. Yankees, Yankee Stadium, Bronx, tel. 293 6000

N. Y. Knicks, Madison Square Garden, Seventh Avenue and   Basketball
32nd Street, tel. 564 4400
N. Y. Nets, Rutgers Center, Piscataway, New Jersey,
tel. 1 (201) 935 8888

Practical Information

Yankee Stadium: Venue of Baseball

Football, American	N. Y. Giants, Giants Stadium, Meadowlands, New Jersey, tel. 1 (201) 935 8222 N. Y. Jets, Shea Stadium, Flushing (Queens), tel. 421 6600
Football, Association	N. Y. Cosmos, Giants Stadium, Meadowlands, New Jersey, tel. 484 6049
Hockey	N. Y. Islanders, Nassau Coliseum, Uniondale (Long Island), tel. (516) 694 5522 N. Y. Rangers, Madison Square Garden, tel. 564 4400
Horse-racing	Aqueduct Racetrack, Ozone Park (Queens), tel. 641 4700 Belmont Raceway, Belmont (Long Island), tel. 641 4700 Meadowlands Racetrack, Meadowlands, New Jersey, tel. 1 (201) 935 8500 Roosevelt Raceway, Westbury (Long Island), tel. 1 (516) 895 3277 Yonkers Raceway, Yonkers, NY, tel. 1 (914) 562 9500
Betting	Bets on horse-races can be placed at offices of the state-sponsored Off-Track Betting Corporation (OTB) which can be found all over the city. Information: tel. 221 5326.

Street names and numbers

Thanks to the regular grid plan adopted by the city fathers in 1811 for the layout of Manhattan N of Washington Square it is easy for visitors to find their way about the city. The streets running up the whole length of Manhattan from S to N are called avenues, those cutting across the island f om E to W are plain streets. The main exception to this regularity is Broadway, Manhattan's longest street, which cuts across the rectangular grid in its course from S to N of the island.

The main avenues are numbered, from First Avenue in the E to Twelfth Avenue in the W, but some bear names, and a few in southern Manhattan are known by letters. The streets are numbered consecutively from S to N. Fifth Avenue divides Manhattan into two parts, East Side and West Side, and the streets E and W of this divide are called, for example, East 42nd Street and West 42nd Street.

The Manhattan avenues are very long, and if you are looking for a particular number it is helpful to know roughly where it is located. This can be achieved by using the following table.

Take the number you are looking for, drop the last digit, divide the remainder by 2 and add or subtract the key number shown against the avenue in the table. The result will give you the number of the cross street nearest the building you are looking for.

First Avenue	+3	Eighth Avenue	+10
Second Avenue	+3	Ninth Avenue	+13
Third Avenue	+10	Amsterdam Avenue	+60
Fourth Avenue	+8	Broadway	−30
Fifth Avenue to 200	+13	(23rd–192nd St)	
201–400	+16	Madison Avenue	+26
401–600	+18	Lexington Avenue	+22
601–775	+20	Central Park West	+60
776–1286	−15	(divide number by 10)	
(do not divide by 2)		Riverside Drive	+72
1287–1500	+45	(divide number by 10)	
Avenue of the	−12	West End Avenue	+60
Americas		Seventh Avenue	+12
Seventh Avenue	+12		
(to 110 St)			

Example: To find the situation of 825 Madison Avenue, drop the final 5 to give 82; divide by 2 to give 41; and add the 26 shown in the table to give 67. Thus 825 Madison Avenue lies at the intersection with 67th Street.

Taxis

There is no difficulty about getting a taxi in Manhattan, except at rush hours and if it is raining. Taxis, which are painted a distinctive yellow, can be hailed in the street if the little glass dome on the roof is illuminated. If a taxi is off duty or on radio call it will not stop.

Taxis can also be called by telephone. The following firms run a 24-hour service:
All City Radio Taxi, tel. 796 1111
Dial-a-Cab, tel. 743 8383
Ding-a-Ling, tel. 691 9191

The fare is one dollar, plus ten cents for each ninth of a mile.

Telegrams

Telegrams are almost invariably telephoned, since there are very few telegraph offices where they can be handed in.

Domestic and international telegrams

Western Union, tel. 962 7111

Cablegrams

ITT Communications, tel. 797 3300
RCA Global Communications, tel. 363 4141

Night letters

These are a cheap and rapid form of communication: for example, 22 words cost $2.92 (plus tax).

Telephone

Dialling codes

New York: 212
To the United Kingdom: 011 44
To Canada: as for a long-distance call within the United States (i.e. dial 0 followed by the local dialling code)

Tariffs

Local calls from coin-operated telephones cost ten cents. Long-distance, and particularly international, calls cannot be dialled from coin-operated telephones, which accept no coins larger than 25 cents. If you have a friend whose telephone you can use this is preferable to telephoning from a hotel, which normally adds a surcharge to the cost of a call. A three-minute call to Europe costs some $6 during the day (direct dialling), rather less in the evening and during the night.

Toll-free calls

Certain numbers (in the form 800 123 4567) can be dialled free of charge (e.g. for hotel reservations, information, etc.). Dial 1, followed by the number.

Television

See Radio and television

Theatres

The theatrical life of New York is rich and varied, and can no longer be thought of merely as Broadway, as it used to be. It is still true, however, that the 40 or so theatres around Broadway and Times Square, between 41st and 53rd Streets, are the ones best known to visitors, who will usually not be in New York long enough to discover the 15 repertory theatres, the 15 "off-Broadway" theatres and the large number (200–250) "off-off-Broadway" theatres. While the Broadway houses specialise in musicals and light pieces, the other theatres largely go in for serious drama, from the Greeks to contemporary playwrights, with particular emphasis on plays by American authors.

Alvin, 250 West 52nd Street, tel. 757 8646
Ambassador, 215 West 49th Street, tel. 541 6490

Barrymore, 243 West 47th Street, tel. 246 0390
Belasco, 111 West 44th Street, tel. 354 4490
Bijou, 209 West 45th Street, tel. 221 8500
Biltmore, 261 West 47th Street, tel. 582 5340
Booth, 222 West 45th Street, tel. 246 5969
Broadhurst, 235 West 44th Street, tel.247 0472
Broadway, 1681 Broadway, tel. 247 7260
Brooks Atkinson, 256 West 47th Street, tel. 245 3430
Cort, 138 West 48th Street, tel. 489 6392
Edison, 240 West 47th Street, tel. 757 7164
Ethel Merman, 226 West 46th Street, tel. 246 4271
Eugene O'Neill, 230 West 49th Street, tel. 246 0220
Gershwin, 1633 Broadway, tel. 586 6510
Golden, 252 West 45th Street, tel. 246 6740
Helen Hayes, 210 West 46th Street, tel. 246 6380
Imperial, 249 West 45th Street, tel. 265 4311
Longacre, 220 West 48th Street, tel. 246 5639
Lunt-Fontanne, 205 West 46th Street, tel. 586 5555
Lyceum, 149 West 45th Street, tel. 582 3897
Majestic, 245 West 44th Street, tel. 246 0730
Mark Hellinger, 237 West 51st Street, tel. 757 7050
Martin Beck, 302 West 45th Street, tel. 246 6363
Minskoff, Broadway and 45th Street, tel. 869 0550
Music Box, 239 West 45th Street, tel. 246 4636
Nederlander, 208 West 41st Street, tel. 391 3999
New Apollo, 234 West 43rd Street, tel. 921 8558
Palace, Broadway and 47th Street, tel. 757 2626
Plymouth, 236 West 45th Street, tel. 730 1760
Rialto, 1481 Broadway, tel. 354 5236
Royale, 242 West 45th Street, tel. 245 5760
St James, 246 West 44th Street, tel. 398 0280
Shubert, 225 West 44th Street, tel. 246 5990
Virginia Theatre, 245 West 52nd Street, tel. 977 9370
Winter Garden, 1634 Broadway, tel. 245 4878

American Place Theater, 111 West 46th Street, tel. 247 0394
Circle in the Square, 1633 Broadway, tel. 581 0720
CSC Repertory Company, 136 East 13th Street, tel. 677 4210
Jean Cocteau Repertory Company, 330 Bowery, tel. 677 0060
LaMama ETC, 74A East 4th Street, tel. 475 7710
Lion Theater Company, 422 West 42nd Street, tel. 947 4224
Manhattan Theater Club, 321 East 73rd Street, tel. 472 0600
Negro Ensemble Company, 424 West 55th Street,
tel. 246 8545
Public Theater, 425 Lafayette Avenue, tel. 677 1750
Roundabout Theater, 333 West 23rd Street, tel. 924 7160
Shelter West, 217 Second Avenue, tel. 673 6341
Theater for the New City, 162 Second Avenue, tel. 254 1109

Repertory theatres

There are also some 12 to 15 off-Broadway theatres which are rented by different companies from time to time (as is also the practice with the Broadway theatres). Like the Broadway theatres, too, they are commercial enterprises.

Off-Broadway theatres

There are between 200 and 250 off-off-Broadway theatres, most of them with fewer than 100 seats. They usually present their shows over an extended weekend, from Thursday to Sunday. The programmes for most of these theatres can be found in "Village Voice" which appears each Wednesday.

Off-off-Broadway theatres

Practical Information

Programmes	To find out what is on, consult the Friday or Sunday editions of the "New York Times" or the other publications mentioned under Events (see entry).
Ticket agencies	Tickets can be bought at theatre box offices or, at the cost of an officially regulated additional charge, from one of the licensed ticket agencies. Among these are: Brown's Theater Ticket Agency, 151 West 51st Street, tel. 581 3795 Embassy Theater Ticket Service, 234 West 50th Street, tel. 757 2204 Leblanc's Theater Tickets, 207 West 45th Street, tel. 757 2300 Manhattan Theater Ticket Service, 1501 Broadway, tel. 582 3600 Tyson Original R. and Co., 266 West 44th Street, tel. 247 7600
"tkts"	On Broadway and 47th Street is a booth labelled "tkts" which sells left-over tickets for the evening's performances at Broadway and some off-Broadway theatres at half price. Open Mon., Tues., Thurs. and Fri. from 3 p.m., Sun., Wed. and Sat. from noon. There is often a queue.
Opera, concerts	See Music

Time

New York observes Eastern Standard Time, which is five hours behind Greenwich Mean Time.
From the last Sunday in April to the last Sunday in October summer time (Eastern Daylight Saving Time), an hour ahead of Eastern Standard Time, is in force.

Tipping

In the United States tips are never included in the form of a service charge on a hotel or restaurant bill, and must be given separately.

Hotels	If your luggage is taken up to your room or brought down from it by a bell-boy: 50 cents per item. Chambermaid: after a stay of some days leave $1–$2 in the room. If the hall-porter gets you a taxi: 50 cents or $1.
Restaurants	Usually 15% of the bill (excluding the 8·25% sales tax). The tip is always left on the table. In better-class restaurants the head waiter ("maître de") also expects a tip.
Taxis	15% of the fare shown on the meter. For a short journey rather more than this may be appropriate.
Hairdressers (men's and women's)	Here too 15% is usual.
Shoe-shine boys	Usually 25 cents.

Tourist information

United States Travel Service, 22 Sackville Street (second floor), London W1X 2EA, tel. (01) 237 2011: personal callers Mon.–Fri. 10 a.m.–4 p.m. Postal enquiries to P.O. Box 2000, London SE1 5JZ.
New York State Tourist Office, 35 Piccadilly, London W1: telephone enquiries (01) 734 7282.

In the United Kingdom

New York Convention and Visitors Bureau, 2 Columbus Circle (ground floor), tel. 397 8222
Open Mon.–Fri. 9 a.m.–6 p.m., Sat. and Sun. 10 a.m.–6 p.m.
Branch office in Times Square (Broadway and 42nd Street), tel. 593 8983
Open daily 9 a.m.–6 p.m.
State of New York Department of Commerce, 230 Park Avenue (8th Floor), tel. 949 0577

In New York

Chinese American Arts Council
Chinese Community Cultural Center
(See A to Z, Chinatown)

Chinatown

The United States Travel Service has a "Visit the USA" Desk which can be called free of charge (800 255 3050, in Kansas 800 322 4350) from anywhere in the United States for information about the country and the people of the United States, travel, dealing with government offices and what to do in case of illness or emergency.

Telephone information

Transport

The New York buses – a considerably slower means of getting from place to place than the subway – run "uptown" and "downtown" services, going respectively from S to N and from N to S, and "crosstown" services going from E to W and from W to E. Most services run round the clock.
The uptown and downtown routes serve almost all the N–S avenues, but since these are one-way streets the uptown route goes along a different avenue from the corresponding downtown route. The crosstown routes follow the principal cross streets, in particular 9th, 14th, 23rd, 34th, 42nd, 50th, 59th, 66th, 72nd, 79th, 86th, 96th, 103rd, 110th, 125th and 135th Streets.
See the plans of bus routes on pp. 162–4.
Bus stops are marked by yellow lines on the pavement; in Manhattan there are plexiglass shelters at many stops.
Passengers get on at the front of the bus and get off at the rear. Smoking is prohibited and dogs (except guide dogs for the blind) are not allowed. If you want to get off, ring the bell before your stop.
There is a flat-rate fare of 75 cents, which is put into a box on entering the bus (no change given: have the exact fare ready, in coins or subway tokens). Children over six pay the full fare.
If you want to change from an uptown or downtown bus to a crosstown bus, or vice versa, ask for a transfer ("Add-a-Ride") ticket (no additional charge).
Information on bus services: tel. 330 1234 (24 hours a day).

Buses

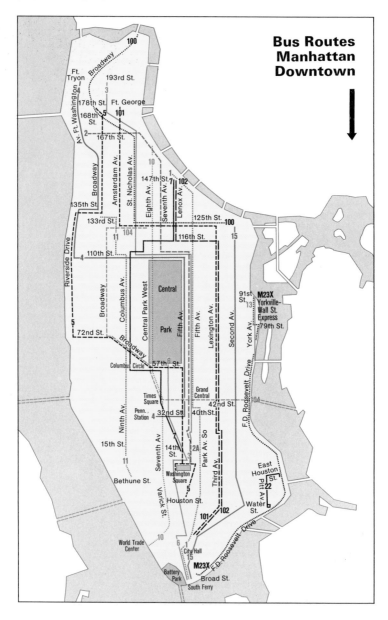

**Bus Routes
Manhattan
Downtown**

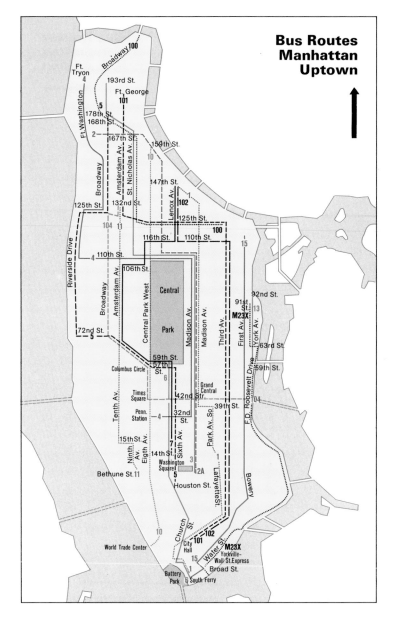

Bus Routes
Manhattan
Uptown

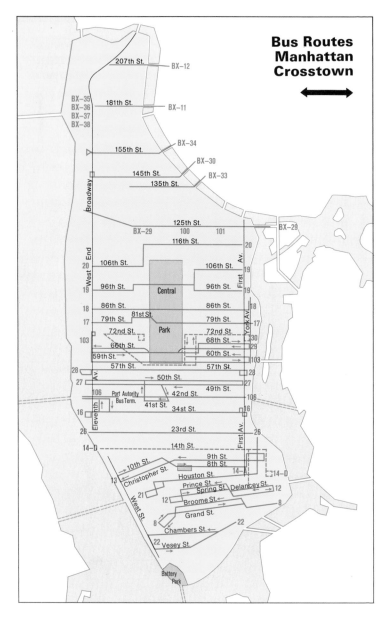

Bus Routes Manhattan Crosstown

207th St. — BX–12

BX–35
BX–36   181st St. — BX–11
BX–37
BX–38

BX–34
155th St.
BX–30
Broadway   145th St.
BX–33
135th St.

125th St.   20
BX–29   100   101   BX–29
116th St.

West End   20   106th St.   106th St.   First Av.   19
19   96th St.   96th St.   19
18   86th St.   Central   86th St.   18
17   79th St.   81st St.   79th St.   17
72nd St.   72nd St.   30
103   66th St.   Park   68th St.   29
59th St.   60th St.   103
57th St.   57th St.   York Av.

28   Av.   28
27   50th St.   27
106   Port Autority   49th St.   106
Bus Term.   42nd St.
41st St.
16   Eleventh   34th St.   First Av.   16
26   23rd St.   26

14–D   14th St.   14–D

9th St.
10th St.   8th St.
13   Christopher St.   Houston St.   14–A   14–D
21   Prince St.   Delancey St.   12
12   Spring St.
Broome St.   8
8   Grand St.
West St.   Chambers St.   22
22   Vesey St.

Battery
Park

The New York subway is one of the world's most complicated underground systems. It was originally run by three companies, one public and two private, which were amalgamated in 1940. There are 23 lines and 462 stations, situated in four of the city's five boroughs; the total length of track is about 350 km (220 miles). Running round the clock, the subway carries over a million passengers every day; and at the rush hours (7.30–9 a.m. and 4.30–7 p.m.) it tends to feel as if the whole million were there at the same time.

There is a map of the subway system on the plan at the end of the Guide. In Manhattan there are subway lines along Eighth Avenue (lines A, AA, CC and E – this last line turning E at 53rd Street and heading for Queens), Seventh Avenue (lines 1, 2 and 3), Broadway (lines N and RR, both turning E at 60th Street for Queens), Avenue of the Americas (lines B, BB, D and F – this last running under 53rd Street to Queens) and Park and Lexington Avenues (lines 4, 5 and 6). All these lines go to Brooklyn. Line 7 runs between Times Square and Flushing (Queens). On almost all the subway lines there are both "express" and "local" trains.

Smoking is prohibited in the trains and on the platforms, and dogs (except guide dogs for the blind) are not allowed.

There is a flat-rate fare of 75 cents. Tokens are sold in subway stations and inserted into a slot in the automatic turnstile: there are no tickets.

Information: tel. 330 1235 (24-hour service).

The "aerial tramway" is a cableway, opened in 1976, between Second Avenue (58th Street) and Roosevelt Island (15-minute service; fare paid by token). This is a temporary arrangement pending the construction of a subway station (lines from Manhattan to Queens along 63rd Street) on this island in East River, which already has a population of over 20,000.

Travel documents

Passports are required by all visitors to the United States except Canadian and British subjects resident in either Canada or Bermuda and returning there from a visit to a country in North, Central or South America. British visitors must have a regular 10-year passport: the one-year British visitor's passport is not valid in the United States.

Every visitor to the United States except Canadian citizens must also have a US visa. Visas, which are valid for more than one visit, can be obtained from US consulates on completion of the appropriate application form. Applications by post should be made at least 3–4 weeks before the expected departure date. In the United Kingdom there are US consulates in:

London
American Embassy
Visa Branch
5 Upper Grosvenor Street
London W1A 2JB

Edinburgh
American Consulate General
3 Regent Terrace
Edinburgh EH7 5BW

Belfast
American Consulate General
Queen House
14 Queen Street
Belfast BT1 6EQ

Universities and colleges

In Manhattan alone there are more than 30 universities and colleges, and in the whole of New York City there are over 50 higher educational establishments. The largest, with over 40,000 students, is New York University; the most respected is Columbia University. Both of these are privately run. Among leading institutions of higher education in Manhattan are the following (listed in alphabetical order):

Bank Street College of Education, 610 West 112th Street, tel. 663 7200
Barnard College, 606 West 120th Street, tel. 284 5265
Bernard Baruch College, 155 East 24th Street, tel. 725 3085
City College of New York, Convent Avenue and 138th Street, tel. 246 9230
City University, 33 West 42nd Street, tel. 790 5345
College of Physicians and Surgeons, 630 West 168th Street, tel. 694 3478
Columbia University, Broadway and 116th Street, tel. 280 1754
Fashion Institute of Technology, 227 West 27th Street, tel. 760 7642
Hunter College, 695 Park Avenue, tel. 570 5118
Jewish Theological Seminary, Broadway and 122nd Street, tel. 749 8000
Juilliard School of Music, 150 West 65th Street, tel. 799 5000
Mount Sinai School of Medicine, Fifth Avenue and 100th Street, tel. 650 6500
New School of Social Research, 66 West 12th Street, tel. 741 5630
New York University, Washington Square, tel. 598 1212
Rockefeller University, York Avenue and 66th Street, tel. 360 1000
School of Visual Arts, 209 East 23rd Street, tel. 679 7350
Teachers' College, 525 West 120th Street, tel. 678 3000
Union Theological Seminary, Broadway and 120th Street, tel. 662 7100
Yeshiva University, Amsterdam Avenue and 185th Street, tel. 960 5400